buffet

parties

delicious party treats and finger food for entertaining

bridget jones

southwater

This edition is published by Southwater

Southwater is an imprint of Anness Publishing Ltd
Hermes House, 88–89 Blackfriars Road, London SE1 8HA
tel. 020 7401 2077; fax 020 7633 9499
www.southwaterbooks.com; info@anness.com

© Anness Publishing Ltd 2004

UK agent: The Manning Partnership Ltd
6 The Old Dairy, Melcombe Road, Bath BA2 3LR
tel. 01225 478444; fax 01225 478440; sales@manning-partnership.co.uk

UK distributor: Grantham Book Services Ltd
Isaac Newton Way, Alma Park Industrial Estate, Grantham, Lincs NG31 9SD
tel. 01476 541080; fax 01476 541061; orders@gbs.tbs-ltd.co.uk

North American agent/distributor: National Book Network
4501 Forbes Boulevard, Suite 200, Lanham, MD 20706
tel. 301 459 3366; fax 301 429 5746; www.nbnbooks.com

Australian agent/distributor: Pan Macmillan Australia
Level 18, St Martins Tower, 31 Market St, Sydney, NSW 2000
tel. 1300 135 113; fax 1300 135 103; customer.service@macmillan.com.au

New Zealand agent/distributor: David Bateman Ltd
30 Tarndale Grove, Off Bush Road, Albany, Auckland
tel. (09) 415 7664; fax (09) 415 8892

A CIP catalogue record for this book is available from the British Library.

A CIP catalogue record for this book is available from the British Library.

Publisher: Joanna Lorenz
Senior Editor: Doreen Palamartschuk
Copy Editors: Jan Cutler, Jane Bamforth
Project Editor: Elizabeth Woodland
Production Controller: Claire Rae
Designer: Nigel Partridge
Jacket Design: Balley Design Associates
Photographers: Karl Adamson, Caroline Arber, Steve Baxter, Martin Brigdale,
Nicki Dowey, Gus Filgate, Michelle Garrett, Amanda Heywood, Janine Hosegood,
William Lingwood, Roisin Neild, Thomas Odulate, Spike Powell, Craig Robertson,
Simon Smith, Sam Stowell and Polly Wreford

Previously published as part of a larger volume, Party Food

10 9 8 7 6 5 4 3 2 1

Notes

Bracketed terms are intended for American readers. For all recipes, quantities are given
in both metric and imperial measures and, where appropriate, measures are also given in standard cups and spoons.
Follow one set, but not a mixture, because they are not interchangeable.
Standard spoon and cup measures are level. 1 tsp = 5ml, 1 tbsp = 15ml, 1 cup = 250ml/8fl oz
Australian standard tablespoons are 20ml. Australian readers should
use 3 tsp in place of 1 tbsp for measuring small quantities of gelatine, flour, salt, etc.
Medium (US large) eggs are used unless otherwise stated.

Contents

Introduction

The brilliance of buffets is that they adapt perfectly to absolutely any event. Buffet tables often appear at those once-in-a-lifetime fabulously formal occasions, but are also perfect for relaxed parties with family and friends. The aim of this book is to provide a wealth of ideas and advice for creating successful buffet parties, for every occasion.

Simply Self-Service

A buffet is the self-service option, providing a variety of snacks and meals. The majority of buffets are ideal for occasions when there will be more guests than seating. The aim is to offer finger food and dishes that can be eaten easily with a fork while standing. However, seating could be created if desired, even if slightly haphazard – soft chairs, floor cushions or *al fresco* on a patio or lawn – allowing guests to cope better with foods that require some cutting or manipulating. If you do have ample seating at set tables, however, it means that the food does not have to be limited to 'fork fare'.

Cold dishes that can be prepared and arranged in advance are convenient. Hot dishes can be kept hot on food warmers or served straight from the oven. Bakes and casseroles are popular, however it is important that these dishes are served promptly to keep them from spoiling.

For sophisticated functions, serving staff or even buffet chefs may be employed to cook, cut or ladle portions of food on to plates. Flambé dishes, griddled and barbecued foods are all ideal for this style of buffet.

Perfect Planning makes the Perfect Party

Achieving a successful party requires planning and detailed list-making. Working lists are efficient and effective. They save time and money, and help to avoid problems. Consider the following when preparing for any party:

- Occasion
- Date, time and venue
- Guests – invitations and replies
- Helpers – family, friends or hired help
- Crockery, cutlery, glasses and linen – disposable, borrowed or hired
- Food – menu and preparation
- Cooking arrangements and storage
- Presentation and garnishes
- Drinks – varieties, quantities and ice
- Entertainment and ambience – type of music, entertainers, decorations and novelties

Left *Colourful canapés are perfect for serving with cocktails and drinks.*

Above *On smaller buffet tables, serve a complementary selection of self-service dishes.*

Buffet Style

Serving food buffet style does not necessarily mean presenting one groaning table of goodies. Arranging food on one long narrow table may be the traditional buffet style for large formal parties held in halls or marquees. However, smaller tables placed in different rooms and spacious hallways are ideal for stylish buffets of different complementary dishes, which can be sampled over several hours rather than as one 'meal'. Snacks, such as tapas, sushi or meze, are perfect served together.

Tables should not be too wide; keep dishes within easy reach of guests. Low tables are fine for finger foods, but can be hazardous for guests when sampling messy dips, or bending over to use serving cutlery.

Dishes, stands and platters of different height, depth and shape make an interesting and accessible arrangement. Stylish labels are useful for identifying unfamiliar foods or vegetarian specialities. It is essential that there is plenty of suitable serving cutlery for the different types of food. Provide tongs, ladles and large spoons that can be easily manipulated one-handed.

Ambience and Enjoyment

When practical decisions are sorted out, relax and take a creative look at decorating the buffet tables to keep with the general party theme or style. Sprinkle with gleaming glitter or table confetti; add glorious bows, swags or swathes of fabric or ribbon; drape with fun decorations and streamers; or remember sparklers for outdoor table decorations – lighting the sparklers is a great way of letting guests know an evening outdoor feast is served. Keep large trimmings below the serving level or well up and behind the food. Make sure the table is well lit and avoid candles or decorations that get in the way of the food.

Most important of all, when the pre-planning is over, smile – the best party atmosphere is the one imparted by a happy and relaxed host or hostess full of fun and energy.

Above *Decorative serving dishes can transform a selection of olives and nuts into a stylish buffet snack.*

Above left *Fruit makes a decorative and fragrant centrepiece on the buffet table.*

Below *An outdoor buffet table can be enhanced with fresh flowers and foliage.*

Shaken and Stirred

Today's drinks party is a celebration of relaxed sophistication. From easy evenings with friends to an opportunity for semi-formal pre- or post-wedding congratulations, sharing drinks and nibbles is sociable. Plan carefully to ensure the occasion flows smoothly.

Setting the scene

Try the following checklist for straightforward drinks party planning. Make lists of all your ideas while you write shopping lists and notes on aspects to organize.
• Define the occasion precisely.
• Focus on the ambience.
• Decide on the type of drinks.
• Select the style of finger food.

Occasion

Drinks party invitations range from "stylishly casual" to "lounge suit and tie" – a balance of relaxed formality in varying proportions. Within this context, define your occasion before making precise plans. For example, a wedding may provide the opportunity for a gathering of friends not invited to the ceremony and main meal, or a celebration with colleagues and

Below *Colourful drinks add to the thrill of the cocktail hour.*

business clients, neighbours or other associates outside your immediate circle of personal friends.

Whatever the occasion, the number of guests and whether you intend inviting one or more groups of people are important. There is no reason why a drinks party should be connected to any particular event – this is precisely the sort of opportunity to catch up with friends or meet and greet acquaintances. The party may be short – lunchtime or pre-dinner – or an open-ended evening. So there is plenty of scope for setting subtle differences in ambience once you have clear aims.

Drinks

Decide on the type of drinks: cocktails, champagne, wine or an open bar. Cocktails are classic pre-dinner drinks. Champagne is always acceptable and perfect when there is a special toast to raise. Red and white wines are a popular choice. Providing an open bar (that is, offering a selection of shorts and mixers, wine or beer) is the most difficult and expensive, but this can be successful for a limited number of guests, especially if you know them well. Always provide mineral water and a good choice of soft drinks as alternatives to alcohol.

Food style

The food should fit the occasion, ambience and drinks. A plentiful supply of chunky and satisfying finger food is ideal for the sort of relaxed drinks party that drifts into late evening. Dainty canapés and cocktail nibbles are sufficient for a short pre-dinner party. Generous quantities of extra-special, stylish finger food go down well on special occasions. Among the myriad of food options, remember bread and cheese; hot fondues and dips; or international savouries, such as Japanese sushi or Spanish tapas.

Above *Arrange nibbles on platters so that guests can easily help themselves.*

Serving snacks

Distribute plates or bowls of snacks around side tables and surfaces (protect surfaces to avoid damage from spills). Offer nibbles as you mingle, or move them near groups of guests and encourage everyone to dip in. Take platters of hot canapés around or enlist the help of a friend or co-host.

Below *Hire a range of different cocktail glasses for an authentic touch.*

Above *Avocado-filled eggs make excellent little canapés.*

Right *A selection of canapés and light bites suitable for a drinks party.*

Planning finger food

For stylish refreshments, present a modest range of excellent items. Select a number of complementary types of food, including variety in colour, texture and flavour. The following examples show how to match crisp and smooth textures and different ingredients and dishes. Broaden the variety by including a range of sandwich, tart or pastry fillings or toppings. In addition to the main snacks, distribute bowls of good quality bought (or home-made) nibbles, such as roasted nuts, breadsticks and Chinese rice crackers.

• Mini open sandwiches, crisp short pastry tartlets, fruit and cheese savouries on sticks, and crudités with dips.

• Filo-wrapped savouries, bread-based canapés, filled salad vegetables, and smoked salmon and/or ham rolls.

• Bitesize pizza pieces, Spanish tortilla squares, miniature fish cakes, cheese or meat croquettes, and crudités.

• Miniature kebabs, fish goujons, dried fruit wrapped in prosciutto, walnuts sandwiched with cream cheese.

• Smoked salmon sandwiches, marinated mini-mozzarella cheese skewered with cherry tomatoes.

• Excellent chocolate truffles.

Making canapés

The trick to making impressive canapés without an army of experts is by adopting a conveyor-belt method.

Buy large square sandwich loaves of white, wholemeal (whole-wheat) or rye bread and leave them unwrapped at room temperature for a day. Trim off the crusts, and then cut each loaf lengthways into large, fairly thin slices. Spread with the chosen topping, such as a savoury butter, flavoured soft cheese, pâté or spread. For speed, use a topping that can be piped, rather than spread, such as soft cheese or creamy mixtures. The bases can be prepared to this stage a day ahead; cover with clear film (plastic wrap) and pack in a plastic bag. Cut into squares or fingers.

Arrange the canapés on serving platters and then add the garnishes. For efficiency, prepare a tray that can be added to the topped canapés quickly and easily.

Fuss-free options include: lumpfish row, peeled cooked tiger prawns (shrimp), stuffed green olives, pecan nut halves, halved cherry tomatoes, halved canned artichoke hearts or peeled and halved cucumber slices.

Portions

The amount guests will eat depends on the time of day and length of the party. The following is a rough guide to the number of bitesize canapés or snacks to prepare for comparatively formal occasions. It is as well to be aware that the more relaxed and lively the gathering, the more people are likely to eat.

• Allow 5 items per person as an appetizer with drinks before a meal.

• Allow 10–12 items per person for an early evening drinks party (assuming that guests will be going on to dinner elsewhere).

• Allow 12–14 items per person for evening refreshments following a late lunch party, wedding breakfast or reception. (Remember to increase this when inviting additional guests in the evening that have not shared the main meal.)

• Allow 14–16 small items per person for light lunchtime or supper refreshments.

at a time, keeping the rest of the pastry covered with clear film (plastic wrap) to prevent it from drying and cracking. Brush with a little melted butter or olive oil, or a mixture of both. Cut the sheet widthways into 7.5cm/3in wide strips.

For fingers, place a little full-flavoured filling across one end of a pastry strip. Fold the end and sides of the strip over, and then roll it up. To make triangles, place a little mound of filling in the middle of the strip about 4cm/1½in from the end. Fold the corner of the pastry and filling over into a triangle across one end, then continue folding the triangle of filling over along the length of the strip.

Perfect pastries

These can be prepared in advance; they are easy to eat, satisfying and versatile. Try the following tips for streamlined preparation:

Puff pastries: prepare three different full-flavoured, well-seasoned cooked fillings. For speedy preparation make squares, triangles and oblong shapes.

Brush the rolled-out pastry lightly with beaten egg before cutting it into 6cm/2½in squares. These can be paired to make square pastries or folded in half into triangles or oblongs. Use one filling for each shape and place a small mound in the appropriate place on

Above *Little pastries, such as piroshki, are always popular party foods.*

each square – centre slightly generous amounts for squares (leave an equal number blank for topping); in one corner for triangles; and to one side for oblongs. Top the squares and fold the others in half. Press the edges together and place on baking sheets. Brush with beaten egg and bake at 220°C/425°F/ Gas 7 for 7–10 minutes, until well puffed and golden. Cool on wire racks.

Flaky filo savouries: filo pastry triangles or fingers are extremely easy and quick to make. Work on one sheet

Kebabs and cocktail-stick snacks

For party finger food, make kebabs and snacks on sticks that are super tasty and neat:

• Thread no more than three miniature items on mini-kebabs.

• Cook trays of marinated ingredients, such as chicken or beef, then cool and thread them on to mini-wooden skewers. Reheat on ovenproof serving platters. Try cubes of chicken or gammon, mini-meatballs, mini-sausages, slices of spicy sausage, squares of (bell) pepper, small pickling onions, halved baby aubergines (eggplant) or cherry tomatoes.

Below *Flaky filo fingers are easy to make for large numbers.*

Below *Leek, saffron and mussel tartlets are tasty finger food.*

Below *Little cheese pies with raisins and pine nuts make great nibbles.*

Filling ideas for pastries

• Mash a 50g/2oz can of sardines in olive oil with the oil from the can, 1 crushed garlic clove, 2 finely chopped spring onions (scallions), the grated rind of 1 lemon, a squeeze of lemon juice, salt and a pinch of chilli powder.

• Mix finely chopped or minced (ground) cooked ham with a little freshly grated Pecorino cheese, a generous dollop of wholegrain mustard and plenty of chopped fresh chives.

• Mix plenty of finely chopped sun-dried tomatoes, pine nuts, a few chopped raisins and a generous pinch of dried oregano into cream cheese.

• Mash feta cheese to fine bread-crumbs and mix with chopped spring onion, a little oregano and enough ricotta cheese to bind the mixture into a paste.

• Mix chopped, well-drained cooked spinach with chopped spring onion, 1 chopped garlic clove (optional), a little freshly grated Parmesan cheese and enough ricotta to make a firm paste. Season with salt, pepper and a little nutmeg.

• Make sure cocktail-stick (toothpick) bites are bitesize rather than too large to pop into the mouth in one go. (Biting savouries off sticks can mean that the piece left on the stick falls off.)

• Strips of tender foods that roll well are good spread with soft cheese or used as wrappers for firm ingredients. Roll smoked halibut or salmon, cured or cooked ham, salami, peeled roasted (bell) peppers or canned pimientos.

• Olives, melon balls, halved cooked baby new potatoes, cubes of

Above *Many supermarkets now sell good-quality prepared sushi.*

cucumber, pieces of dried fruit (prunes, apricots or dates) and radishes are tasty wrapped in cooked or cured meat.

Simply stylish sushi

Sushi is delicious and practical as it can be prepared ahead, arranged on platters, covered and chilled. Ideally, make the sushi a few hours in advance; however, it can be prepared the day before. Keep it well wrapped to prevent the rice from hardening. Remove from the refrigerator about 30 minutes before serving.

• Rolled sushi: buy mini-sheets of toasted and seasoned nori seaweed to make cocktail-sized rolled sushi rice. Top with dressed cooked sushi rice and add two or three strips of ingredients such as cucumber, spring onion (scallion), cooked carrot or cooked dried shiitake mushrooms marinated in soy sauce and a little sherry. Roll up firmly and neatly. Wrap each roll in clear fim (plastic wrap), twisting the ends firmly. Cut into small pieces before serving.

• Mini-moulded sushi: shape mini-sushi squares by pressing the dressed, cooked rice into ice cube trays. Place a small square of smoked salmon, smoked halibut, thin omelette or thinly sliced smoked or marinated tofu in the bottom of each ice cube compartment before pressing in the rice and topping each one with another square of the same or a piece of nori. Unmould on to a board and top with a suitable garnish, such as lumpfish roe, quartered cucumber slices and/or pieces of pickled ginger. Serve with small bowls of wasabi or light soy dipping sauce.

Below *Butterfly prawn (shrimp) spiedini with chilli and raspberry dip.*

Fabulous Fork Food

Formal or casual, this type of food is fun to prepare, simple to serve and effortless to eat. Make light of the planning by adopting a completely practical approach to this style of buffet instead of stretching it beyond its limits.

Menu options

The fork buffet menu may be for a two- or three-course meal, laid out in stages, or a series of complementary refreshments presented together. Display a menu to let guests know what to expect and to encourage self-service. Although food must be complementary and marry well to form a meal if that is the intention, a party buffet is an occasional treat, so well-balanced nutritional value is not necessarily a priority.

Below *Cut large tarts into slices so that they are easy to eat with just a fork.*

When offering a first course, serve it from a separate side table before placing main dishes on the buffet to avoid any confusion over what should be eaten first. When serving a comparatively small number (10–20 guests) it may be easier to present the first course served on small plates, with accompanying cutlery. These can be arranged on a side table or handed around from trays.

For a stylish main course, focus on one or two main dishes and add easy-to-eat main accompaniments, such as creamy mashed potatoes, rice, pasta or couscous. To avoid overflowing plates, limit the number of vegetable or salad accompaniments to one or two that really make the most of the main dish.

When serving a range of savoury refreshments rather than a traditionally well-balanced main course, select dishes that are contrasting rather than complementary. However, avoid

Above *Tomato and courgette timbale is a light dish and ideal fork food.*

clashing flavours as guests often sample a little of each dish instead of eating just one or two.

Desserts are not likely to be confused with the main course, so they can be arranged towards the back of the buffet table to be moved forward when the main dishes have been cleared away.

Cheese can be seen as an alternative to main dishes, so if you want it strictly as a separate course, set the cheese board and accompaniments on a side table away from the main buffet.

Practical fork food

There is nothing worse than doing battle with food that is difficult to eat while balancing a glass and trying to make conversation.

• Serve ingredients in small pieces or that can be broken easily with the side of a fork.

• Select foods and dishes that cling together well and are easily scooped up on a fork.

• While moist dishes are successful, excess thin sauce can be difficult to eat and will drip easily.

• Match dishes or ingredients with complementary sauces or dressings

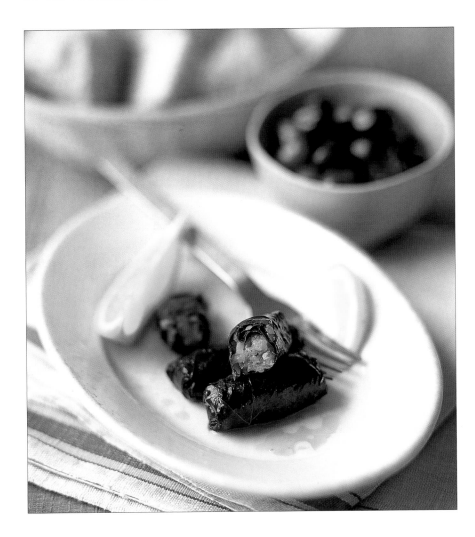

Above *Stuffed vine leaves can be home-made or bought from the deli.*

rather than serving a main dish and accompaniments in different sauces that clash or are too runny.

Favourite foods

The following dishes are always popular and are easy to serve:
• Pasta bakes, such as lasagne and cannelloni. Try fillings with seafood, poultry, vegetable or ricotta cheese as alternatives to meat.
• Dishes full of bitesize chunks in lightly thickened sauces – lamb or chicken curries, boeuf à la bourguignonne, beef casseroles, coq au vin made with boneless chunks of chicken, ratatouille.
• Comforting mince (ground beef) dishes – chilli con carne, moussaka and bitesize meatballs in tomato sauce.
• Moreish rice dishes, such as creamy risotto, slightly spicy kedgeree and rice

salad with a fine yet light, slightly creamy dressing.
• Creamy potato salad, fine-cut coleslaw, tomato and mozzarella salad made with halved cherry tomatoes.

Below *Savoury rice dishes are easily eaten with just a fork.*

Stylish options
Add one or two stylish variations to a fork supper. Try one of the following:
• Savoury moulds and creamy mousses, such as seafood or vegetable terrines, fish or seafood mousses, tender foods or eggs in aspic.
• Dressed salmon, Coquille St. Jacques or other seafood gratins.
• International specialities such as a saffron risotto with shredded Parma ham and basil, seafood paella or spicy Moroccan-style tagine.

Desserts
These are often overlooked for informal fork buffets: this is unfortunate because their are plenty of options. Individual pots or dishes are easy to eat but they do take up space. Large items that cut easily or can be spooned out are most practical.
• Fruit salads, mousses and fools.
• Filo pastries with soft cheese, nut, fruit or chocolate fillings.
• Superlative trifle, light-as-air meringues, luscious chocolate desserts.
• Miniature portions of desserts, such as cheesecake, individual gâteaux, bitesize shortcake or tiny fruit tarts.

Below *Fresh feta cheese, good quality olives and bread are excellent party fare.*

Dinner from the **Buffet**

Balance dinner-party formality with self-service simplicity by offering a traditional menu buffet style. This is an excellent way of sharing a special meal with a larger number of guests than you would normally want to invite to dinner. The ambience can be stylish, with attractively garnished food, elegant table settings and all the trimmings that make memorable celebrations, but without the need for close attention from host or hostess during the meal. A buffet is a good way to entertain whether in a hired room or in a marquee erected at home.

Table tips

Lay out a buffet table to one side of the dining room or in a separate area – this may be another adjacent room, hallway or dining area within the kitchen. Prepare a separate side table for dessert, if necessary, and have the cheese course set out ready for self-service or to be taken to the table when appropriate. Allow room for guests to walk past the buffet without disrupting others seated at the table. Plan the "flow" of guests, arranging food to encourage logical movement in one direction. Prepare a discreet table, trolley or area on which to deposit used plates from the first and main courses, remembering to include a suitable container to take cutlery.

Set the dining table or several different dining tables – a conservatory, hallway or patio can be used instead of, or as well as, the usual dining area. When preparing several tables, take care to arrange them so that they are linked without any one being isolated.

Select a cold first course that can be plated and placed on the tables before guests sit down. Have table heaters, if necessary, for hot main-course dishes, so that they can be arranged on the buffet before guests sit down to the appetizer.

Simple dishes ensure success

The food does not have to be fork friendly – everyone will be sitting down to eat – but it should be approachable for self-service.

• A main course made up of individual portions looks neat and attractive, and

Below Make sure there are plenty of napkins on or near the buffet table.

Above Choose a selection of dishes that are suitable for self-service.

guests will not be intimidated by having to cut or carve. Individual pastries, fish steaks or rolled fillets, or chicken breast portions are typical.

• Casseroles made up of evenly cut ingredients are a good choice.

• Select dishes that can be kept hot successfully without spoiling. Sauced portions or wrapped ingredients that will not dry out easily are the best choices. Pan-fried or freshly grilled items that have to be served freshly cooked are best avoided.

• Instead of plain cooked vegetable accompaniments, select a gratin, purée, casserole or bake that will stay hot without spoiling.

• Bowls of refreshing complementary side salad can be placed on the dining table after the first course.

• Cold salsas, sauces or condiments for main dishes can be placed on the dining table.

• Platters of individual desserts look elegant and are easy to serve – try making individual versions of large recipes, such as little fruit tarts, mini-gâteaux, meringue pairs, little choux pastries and individual mousses or moulded sweets.

Menu reminders

Remember the usual rules for creating good menus: go for complementary flavours, contrasting textures and appealing colours. In addition, when serving the food buffet-style consider the following ideas:

• Easy appetizers: arrange stylish portions of salads that will not wilt on individual plates at the table. Try marinated roasted vegetables and mini or cubed cheese; cured meats with olives, Parmesan flakes and crusty bread; little cheese or vegetable mousses with crisp savoury biscuits (crackers); home-made fish or meat pâté with tiny dinner rolls; smoked salmon marinated with chopped fresh dill and mustard in olive oil; or pickled herring with shredded cooked beetroot (beet) and horseradish.

• Simple-to-serve main dishes: cubed boneless chicken or turkey breast; venison, beef, lamb or pork all make delicious casseroles enriched with wine and spirits; or cook breast fillets of chicken, turkey, pheasant or duck in wine sauces reduced to a thin glaze for coating. Cook boneless portions of fish, poultry or meat in filo or puff pastry, adding herb butter before wrapping. Game, poultry or vegetarian pies are suitable for formal and informal buffet meals, and whole cooked salmon is always popular.

• No-fuss accompaniments: simple leafy salads with dressings served on the side; creamy mashed potatoes flavoured with herbs, garlic, spring onions (scallions) and olives; roasted mixed vegetables dressed with citrus

Above *Whole meat joints can be carved and served at the buffet.*

rind and herbs after cooking; vegetable gratins; or casseroles of Mediterranean vegetables, such as ratatouille.

• So to dessert: for an elegant statement, make a simple salad of two or three fruits with an intriguing hint of additional flavour – try mango and raspberry dressed with orange juice and a little honey; strawberry and papaya with a hint of lime rind and

Above *Home-made truffles make a wonderful finishing touch to any party.*

juice; chilled pears poached in cider with melon and chopped preserved stem ginger; or pineapple marinated with cardamom and sprinkled with coconut. Classic individual dishes, such as crème caramel or crème brûlée and meringue nests, are all good for a buffet.

Below *Contrasting colours and textures provide an appetizing display.*

Just Nibbles

Tune in the party by serving the right type and quantity of snacks with drinks when guests first arrive. Too few or poor quality nibbles look mean and awkward; too many or filling snacks overfill guests before the meal. Flavours should preview the courses to follow; for example, it is not good form to serve powerful, spicy snacks before a delicate meal.

Off-the-shelf selection
The array makes it difficult to resist trying some of the amazing commercial creations, but it is best to do this in your non-entertaining time. Select plain snacks and classic products rather than bizarre concoctions. Many bought savouries are wildly over-seasoned and they completely dull the palate for a delicate meal. Plain salted nuts, Chinese-style rice crackers, simple breadsticks, lightly flavoured croûtons, and good quality crisps (US potato chips) and cocktail crackers complement home-made snacks.

Roasted nuts
Place blanched almonds and plain, shelled pistachio and macadamia nuts in a large, shallow ovenproof dish. Sprinkle with a little salt and cook at 200°C/400°F/Gas 6 for about 6–10 minutes, or until pale golden. Shake the dish well to coat the nuts with the salt and leave to cool. For a deliciously elusive hint of spice, sprinkle the nuts with two or three pinches each of grated nutmeg and ground mace.

Below *Pistachio nuts, almonds and macadamia nuts are good party snacks.*

Below *Feta cheese with roast pepper dip with chillies on toast.*

Above *Good-quality bread, cheese, olives and wine are essential party basics.*

Marinated olives
Lightly crumple 4 bay leaves and place in a small pan with 15ml/1 tbsp fennel seeds, the grated rind of 1 lemon and 2 peeled and sliced garlic cloves. Pour in a little olive oil and cook gently for 15 minutes so that the ingredients barely sizzle. Remove from the heat and whisk in the juice of 1 lemon, 5ml/1 tsp caster (superfine) sugar and a little salt and pepper. Stir in 250ml/8fl oz/1 cup olive oil. Drain a 250g/9oz can pitted black olives in brine, then add them to the oil and mix well. Transfer to a covered container and leave to marinate in the refrigerator for 2–7 days. Drain the olives before serving. (The oil is fabulous for dressing cured meats, vegetables and salads.)

Marinated cheese

Prepare the marinade used for olives to flavour bitesize cubes of feta cheese or mini-mozzarella cheeses. The fennel seeds are good with the cheese but they can be omitted and replaced by several sprigs of fresh oregano instead. Alternatively, instead of fennel and oregano, sprinkle the drained cheese with finely shredded basil when serving. Gouda or Jarlsberg cheese is excellent soaked in the same marinade with fennel, cumin or caraway seeds.

Vegetable crisps

Home-made potato crisps are special when combined with other vegetables, such as beetroot (beet), sweet potatoes, celeriac and carrots.

Peel and thinly slice the potatoes and/or vegetables using a hand peeler, food processor or mandolin. Rinse well in cold water, drain and dry thoroughly on clean dishtowels. Make sure all the slices are separate before deep-frying a handful at a time in hot oil until they

Below Lemon and herb marinated olives are tasty party nibbles.

are crisp and golden. Drain thoroughly on paper towels and season lightly with salt.

Roasted cardamom cauliflower florets

Split 8 green cardamom pods and heat gently in a large pan with 60ml/4 tbsp sunflower oil until the pods are just sizzling, then cook for 2 minutes. Break a trimmed cauliflower into bitesize florets. Add the florets to the pan and toss to coat thoroughly in the oil, then turn them out into a shallow ovenproof dish, scraping all the oil over them. Roast at 220°C/425°F/Gas 7 for 10

Above Spiced plantain chips with hot chilli sauce.

minutes, turning once, until lightly browned. Season lightly and cool. Discard the cardamoms when transferring the cauliflower florets to serving bowls.

Baguette croûtons

Cut a good baguette with good, soft centre crumb into quarters lengthways. Cut the quarters across into large bitesize chunks. Spread these out in a large roasting pan and bake at 160°C/325°F/Gas 3 for about 40 minutes, turning occasionally, until crisp, dry and lightly browned. Finely chop 1 garlic clove and cook lightly in 30ml/2 tbsp olive oil for 1 minute. Add 5ml/1 tsp each of dried oregano and thyme, then pour in a further 60ml/4 tbsp olive oil. Heat gently for a few minutes, then trickle evenly and thinly over the croûtons. Season lightly with salt and toss well, then return to the oven for a further 5 minutes. Toss with plenty of finely chopped fresh parsley and finely grated lemon rind, if you like, just before serving.

For lightly flavoured croûtons, heat 2 bay leaves, a blade of mace and the pared rind of 1 lemon with the oil instead of the garlic, oregano and thyme. Leave to stand for several hours before pouring over the croûtons.

Salsas, Dips and Dippers

A few good salsas and dips go a long way, and a repertoire of basic recipes can be varied to create exciting snacks. Try them as fillings for hollowed vegetables or halved hard-boiled eggs; spread them on soft tortillas, wraps or pancakes and roll up into tasty picnic snacks or slice them into stylish canapés.

Matching dippers to dips

Vegetable crudités, breadsticks, croûtes and crackers taste good with most dips. For a juicy dip, select dippers to scoop up and hold juice or absorb a little – thick, curly crisps (US potato chips) and tortilla chips work well.

Below *Crunchy tacos are perfect with tomato salsa and guacamole.*

Do's and don'ts for dips and dippers

Do …
• Make smooth, fairly soft, but not sloppy, dips for easy eating.
• Select sturdy and fairly short nibbles to dunk – chunky lengths of celery, carrot, (bell) pepper and fennel; mini breadsticks; pitta bread fingers and crackers.
• Use cocktail sticks (toothpicks) for small, firm bits to dunk.
• Match dippers to dips.
• Serve dips in small bowls on platters, surrounded by enough dippers for the entire bowlful of dip.

Don't …
• Make the dip too thick to scoop easily.
• Prepare dips that separate or become watery on standing.
• Serve fragile dippers that break or bend; avoid fine crisps (US potato chips), fine puff pastries and flopping wedges of pitta.
• Offer nibbles that are too small to dunk without putting your fingers into the dip.
• Serve a huge bowl of dip that does the rounds for 30 minutes only to become messy.
• Offer dressed or sauced dunks that discolour and flavour the dip.

• For crisp potato wedges cut medium to large potatoes into quarters lengthways and place in a plastic bag. Add a little sunflower oil and salt, and then mix well. (Add a generous pinch of dried oregano or rosemary if appropriate for the dip.) Turn out into a roasting pan and cook at 240°C/ 475°F/Gas 9 for about 40 minutes, turning two or three times, until crisp and browned. Serve freshly cooked.

These can be three-quarters cooked in advance, then finished in the oven at the last minute. Sweet potatoes and new potatoes also work well.

• For crisp skins, halve baked potatoes and scoop out the middle, leaving a fairly thick shell. Brush all over with oil, place in a greased roasting pan and season lightly with salt. Roast at 200°C/400°F/Gas 6 for about 30 minutes, or until crisp and browned.

Red salsa

Play with this basic mixture to impress your personality on it and excite your palate – add a little extra sugar or chilli, perhaps, and increase the paprika for a deeper, warmer flavour. To lighten the salsa and add a lively zing, omit the tomato purée (paste) and stir in a little lemon juice. The salsa complements fish, poultry, meat or cheese; it makes a terrific dip with fingers of pitta bread or cheese cubes on sticks; and it is delicious on bitesize croûtes, topped with halved, hard-boiled quails' eggs.

Mix 60ml/4 tbsp tomato purée, 1 finely chopped red onion, 1 seeded and finely chopped red (bell) pepper, 1 seeded and finely chopped mild red chilli, 1 crushed garlic clove, 10ml/2 tsp caster (superfine) sugar, 2.5ml/½ tsp paprika and 30ml/2 tbsp balsamic vinegar until thoroughly combined. Peel and chop 450g/1lb ripe tomatoes, then stir them into the mixture. Add salt and pepper to taste. Cover and chill for 1–3 days in the refrigerator.

Cucumber and avocado salsa

This fresh, lively salsa complements fish and seafood, salami and cured meats, and grilled (broiled) and barbecued meats and burgers. It enlivens creamy cheeses. As a dip, it is wicked with potato wedges or skins, and chunky cheese straws.

Peel and finely chop 1 cucumber, then place it in a sieve. Sprinkle with

Below *Tomato-based salsas are very versatile: add chillies, coriander or garlic.*

salt and leave over a bowl to drain for 30 minutes. Meanwhile, finely chop 1 large seeded green (bell) pepper, 1 seeded mild green chilli, 1 bunch of spring onions (scallions) and mix with 15ml/1 tbsp caster sugar, 45ml/3 tbsp good olive oil and the grated rind and juice of 1 lime. Squeeze the cucumber and then dry it on kitchen paper before adding it to the salsa. Halve, stone (pit) and finely chop 2 avocados, then mix them into the salsa. Chop a big bunch of coriander (cilantro) leaves and stir them into the salsa.

Cover and chill for several hours or up to 1 day. Before serving, finely shred a handful of tender basil sprigs and stir them in.

Below *Pitta bread makes excellent dippers for creamy dips.*

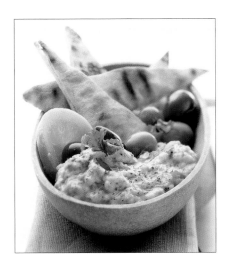

Above *Spicy pumpkin dip served with cucumber crudités.*

Onion and chive dip

This is delicious as a filling for baked potatoes or with crispy barbecue-cooked new potatoes; it is a good accompaniment for baked gammon or a filling for cherry tomatoes.

Peel and quarter 6 onions. Mix 15ml/1 tbsp sugar, 15ml/1 tbsp wholegrain mustard, 30ml/2 tbsp sunflower oil and 30ml/2 tbsp cider vinegar in a shallow ovenproof dish just large enough to hold the onions. Turn the onions in this mixture, then roast at 200°C/400°F/Gas 6 for about 45 minutes, turning once or twice, until tender. Cover and cool.

Purée the onions with their juices. Gradually stir the onion purée into 450g/1lb curd cheese. Finely snip a handful of chives into the dip, add a little freshly grated nutmeg and mix well. Taste for seasoning, then chill.

Gorgonzola and parsley dip

Mash 225g/8oz Gorgonzola cheese and mix in 225g/8oz/1 cup ricotta cheese. Finely chop 50g/2oz flat leaf parsley and mix it into the dip with freshly ground black pepper. Stir in 250ml/8fl oz/1 cup crème fraîche and seasoning to taste. Chill before serving.

Salad Talk

In a flurry of curly leaves or a frisée of fine shreds, every salad should make a stunning statement. Move on from making irrelevant "side salads" to presenting classy creations by marrying vegetables with taste bud-tingling dressings and well-textured toppings.

Salad reminders

Harmonize all aspects of a salad; the base, main ingredients, dressing and topping or garnish should contrast and blend to perfection.

• Include a limited selection of complementary flavours and textures rather than a mishmash of ingredients – this is especially relevant with rice or pasta salads.

• Dress leafy salads at the last minute, otherwise they become limp. For buffets, serve the dressing separately.

• Sprinkle crisp or crunchy toppings over when serving, or offer them separately for buffets.

• Have a generous taste of the dressing to check the seasoning and balance of

Below *Classic Caesar salad is a popular party dish.*

sweet to sour. The dressing must complement not mask the salad.

• There should be enough dressing to coat but not drown the ingredients.

• Light-textured and thin dressings complement soft and crisp ingredients; crunchy and firm ingredients support creamy coatings.

• Unless they should be served chilled, remove salads from the refrigerator about 30 minutes before serving.

Full-of-flavour leaves

The palate-cleansing properties of fresh leaves are welcome with firm, substantial main dishes, such as grilled poultry or meat and hearty raised pies or pastries. They are also an excellent base for sautéed or grilled fish and seafood, finely sliced cured meats or crumbly or creamy cheeses.

For exciting leafy ensembles mix green flavours with subtly different textures. Crisp iceberg, cos or romaine lettuces contrast with lamb's lettuce, lollo rosso or Little Gem (Bibb) leaves.

Baby spinach brings a firm, rather than crisp, texture and a subtle, slightly musty flavour. Peppery watercress and savoury rocket (arugula) bring positive textures as well as lively flavour.

Above *Olive oil and ripe black olives add plenty of flavour.*

Herb sprigs are excellent in leafy salads, either singly or in a burst of mixed flavours. Chopping the herbs changes the result completely, distributing their flavour rather than providing the occasional interesting mouthful; so include small sprig ends with their tender edible stems.

Salad portions

Estimating salad portions for large gatherings is not easy; simply multiplying portion sizes for a meal for four or six by a larger number for a buffet does not work. Portion sizes are smaller for buffet salads. As a rough guide for gatherings of over 20, 1 large lettuce (lollo rosso, iceberg, cos or romaine) will provide eight portions, 500g/1¼lb tomatoes will be enough for six, 1 small white cabbage will serve 12 when finely shredded, 500g/1¼lb new potatoes will serve four and 500g/1¼lb shredded carrots will serve six to eight.

The crunch factor

The greater resistance of crunch is different from crisp and it is a texture that supports substantial ingredients and flavours or creamy dressings very well. Fennel, celery, radishes, cucumber, carrots, celeriac, red or white cabbage, courgettes (zucchini), (bell) peppers, beansprouts and onions are packed with crunch. For super-crunchy salads, add drained and thinly sliced canned water chestnuts.

Tender not soft

Cooked root vegetables, tomatoes, mushrooms, canned bamboo shoots and olives are examples of tender ingredients that can be marinated in dressings to impart or absorb flavours. A suitable marinade should not spoil their textures but it will enrich the salad and give it depth.

Tip-top finishes

The decorative garnishes or toppings for salad add vital flavour and introduce interesting textures.
• Chopped, slivered or whole nuts can complement main ingredients or be a focal point. Walnuts, pecans, pistachios, macadamia nuts and hazelnuts are all excellent on salads.
• Lightly roasted seeds bring strength of flavour and texture. Linseeds, pumpkin, sesame, sunflower, mustard and poppy seeds are all delicious individually or together. Pine nuts are delicious, tender and nutty and go especially well with spinach.
• Lightly roasted grains bring texture and flavour, and they go well with seeds and/or bacon. Barley, rye and/or oat flakes can all be roasted in a dry, heavy pan until lightly browned and crisp.
• Croûtons bring crunch and they can be tasty with herbs and/or garlic.
• Crisp sautéed diced bacon or gammon, salami or chorizo are full of flavour and texture.

Above *White beans with green peppers in a spicy dressing.*

Asides to centrepieces

Salads make appealing first courses or light main courses and many are just a twist away from becoming impressive centrepieces for picnics or buffets. The trick is to marry punchy main ingredients with a salad base full of character, then link them with a sympathetic dressing. Experiment with the following examples:
• A substantial full-flavoured leaf and herb base is brilliant for pan-fried fish, poultry, cheese or tofu. Sliced scallops, peeled raw tiger prawns (shrimp), chunks of salmon, strips of chicken or turkey breast fillet, cubes of halloumi cheese or firm tofu can all be marinated with a little olive oil, garlic and lemon rind, then pan-fried and tossed into the salad while hot. Deglaze the pan with lemon juice or balsamic vinegar, a sprinkling of sugar, seasoning and a final drizzle of olive oil to make a delicious dressing. To serve the salad cold, transfer the pan-fried ingredients to a container, pour over the deglazed dressing and cool, then mix with the leaves before serving.
• Use shredded crunchy salad in a light oil-based dressing as a base for ruffles of thinly sliced cured meats; julienne of cooked meats; quartered hard-boiled eggs and diced smoked salmon or ham; or diced firm cheese. Add a creamy dressing and crunchy topping.
• A mixture of soft and crisp, lightly flavoured leaves (for example lollo biondo, lamb's lettuce and shredded iceberg) is a good base for fresh fruit, rich dried fruit and creamy cheese. Crisp and juicy green grapes, sliced dried apricots and sliced ripe Brie combine well. Add a topping of coarsely chopped walnuts and dress with a drizzle of walnut oil. Add lemon wedges as a little zest to taste.

Below *Refreshing tabbouleh with masses of chopped fresh herbs.*

Sauces, Dressings and Relishes

A good home-made sauce elevates plain cooked foods to a stylish dish. Here are a few classic recipes:

Tomato sauce

This good basic sauce freezes well. Thaw it for several hours at room temperature or in the microwave. Apart from the myriad of uses in compound dishes, the sauce goes well with plain cooked fish, poultry or meat.

For the simplest informal supper party, serve fresh pasta with tomato sauce, topped with lots of finely shredded fresh basil and coriander (cilantro), and shavings of Parmesan cheese. Add a punchy, crunchy salad of shredded fennel and white cabbage with chopped spring onion (scallion) and toasted pine nuts.

Chop 1 onion, 1 celery stick, 1 carrot and 1 garlic clove, then cook in 30ml/2 tbsp olive oil with 2 bay leaves and 1 large sprig each of fresh thyme and oregano for 15 minutes. Cover the pan to keep the moisture in and prevent the vegetables from browning. Add 1kg/2lb chopped ripe tomatoes, 30ml/2 tbsp tomato purée

Below *Pickles add full flavour to accompaniments and condiments.*

(paste), 15ml/1 tbsp sugar, 2.5ml/½ tsp paprika and a little seasoning. Heat, stirring, until the tomatoes give up some of their juice, and simmer then cover the pan and cook gently for 40–45 minutes, until the vegetables are tender and the tomatoes reduced. Discard the bay leaves and herb sprigs, then purée the sauce. Use the sauce as it is (slightly coarse) or press it through a fine sieve for a smooth texture.

Mayonnaise

Home-made mayonnaise is superb, and the flavour can be fine-tuned to your personal taste by adjusting the balance of sunflower and olive oils (or using different types of oil) and the quantity of lemon juice.

Home-made mayonnaise contains raw egg; pregnant women, the very young and the elderly are generally advised not to eat raw eggs.

Commercial mayonnaise, however, is pasteurized to destroy any micro-organisms in the egg and it can be a safer option for buffet dishes that are likely to be left sitting for several hours in a warm room.

Below *Home-made garlic mayonnaise with crudités.*

Above *Home-made mayonnaise is quick to make and so delicious.*

Use an electric beater to whisk 1 large (US extra large) egg with a little salt and pepper, 2.5ml/½ tsp Dijon mustard and the juice of ½ small lemon, until thoroughly combined. Mix 150ml/¼ pint/⅔ cup each of sunflower and olive oil. Whisking constantly, gradually add the oils to the egg in a very thin trickle, broken at first, then more constantly as the mixture thickens and becomes creamy. The finished mayonnaise should be thick, pale and glossy. Add salt, pepper and lemon juice to taste if required.

• The mayonnaise can be made in a food processor by processing the egg mixture first, then gradually dropping and trickling in the oil with the motor running. Scrape the mixture down frequently. A large food processor bowl may be too large for a single quantity.

• For a rich mayonnaise, use egg yolks rather than whole egg and allow 2 egg yolks to 250 ml/8 fl oz/1 cup oil.

Flavouring mayonnaise

A well-flavoured mayonnaise can be served as a filling for baked potatoes or a dip with potato wedges.

• Add 1 crushed garlic clove to the egg. For a mellow flavour, first cook 1 garlic clove in a little olive oil until lightly browned.

• Stir in 60ml/4 tbsp chopped fresh chives, parsley, tarragon, dill or fennel, or a handful of shredded basil leaves.

• Stir in the grated rind of 1 lemon, lime or orange. Use the juice of 1 lime instead of the lemon juice. (Orange juice is not sharp enough to balance the oil and egg mixture.)

• To make a spicy rouille, add 1 crushed garlic clove, 5ml/1 tsp paprika and a good pinch of cayenne pepper to the egg. Taste the prepared mayonnaise for seasoning and add a little extra cayenne if you like. Rouille is a traditional accompaniment for fish soups, served with slices of warm baguette, but it also goes with a wide variety of other foods or it makes a delicious dip for plain breadsticks.

Excellent salad dressing

This is a good basic oil and vinegar salad dressing, which can be varied to suit all sorts of salads. Different types of oil (sunflower, grapeseed, walnut, hazelnut or pumpkin seed) or vinegar (remember all the flavoured vinegars) can be used, and there are many types of mustard that will vary the flavour. Strong nut oils should be used in modest amounts with light grapeseed or sunflower oil.

Below Herbs, garlic or lemon rind can enliven a plain salad dressing.

Above *Quail's eggs served with mayonnaise dip and olive oil.*

Whisk 5ml/1 tsp sugar, salt and freshly ground black pepper, and 7.5ml/1½ tsp mustard (wholegrain or Dijon, mild or strong to taste) with 30ml/2 tbsp balsamic or cider vinegar until the sugar and salt have dissolved. Whisking hard and constantly, slowly pour in 150ml/¼ pint/⅔ cup olive oil. The dressing will emulsify and thicken slightly. Store in an airtight jar in the refrigerator and shake before serving.

Flavouring dressings

Try some of the following additions.

• Add 1 chopped garlic clove.

• Add 30ml/2 tbsp chopped parsley, mint, tarragon or chives.

• Add the grated rind of ½–1 lemon.

• To make a spicy peanut dressing, omit the mustard and use 30ml/2 tbsp crunchy peanut butter. Add the juice of 1 lime and a pinch of dried red chillies.

Beetroot relish

This sweet and sour preserve is terrific with hot or cold meats or with cheese. Serve it with a Christmas buffet or a summer barbecue.

Peel and coarsely grate 450g/1lb raw beetroot (beet). Peel, core and coarsely grate 450g/1lb cooking apples.

Finely chop 450g/1lb onions. Peel and chop 25g/1oz fresh root ginger. Mix all the ingredients in a pan and add 2 crushed garlic cloves, 5ml/1 tsp each of ground cinnamon and nutmeg, 225g/ 8oz/1 cup soft brown sugar and 450ml/ ¾ pint/scant 2 cups cider vinegar. Bring to the boil, stirring occasionally, then reduce the heat and cover the pan. Simmer the relish for about 1½ hours. Pot the relish in warmed sterilized jars immediately the pan is removed from the heat. Cover with airtight lids and store for at least 2 weeks before eating. It makes about 1.3kg/3lb.

Below *Beetroot relish.*

Making the Best of Bread

The advantage of baking your own bread is that you can create individual rolls or loaves to complement the menu or to become a real feature on their own, especially for breakfast, brunch, lunch or late suppers. Breads can be baked or bought well in advance and frozen. Seek out interesting breads and discover lots of ways of using them.

• Wholemeal bread: use wholemeal (whole-wheat) flour and add an extra 50ml/2fl oz/¼ cup water.

• Seeded breads: use all wholemeal or half and half wholemeal and white. Add 15ml/1 tbsp each of caraway and cumin seeds, and 30ml/2 tbsp each of poppy and sesame seeds.

• Rye bread: use half rye flour and half white flour. Add 30ml/2 tbsp caraway seeds and an extra 50ml/2fl oz/¼ cup water to the mixture.

Below *For a party, buy interesting bread flavoured with seeds and herbs.*

• Milk bread: use hand-hot milk instead of water for richer bread. Rub 50g/2oz/¼ cup butter into the flour before adding the yeast, salt and sugar then omit the olive oil. Do not glaze the bread before baking.

• Herb bread: add 10ml/2 tsp dried sage, 10ml/2 tsp dried thyme and 60ml/4 tbsp chopped fresh chives to the flour. Also try oregano, dill, fennel, coriander (cilantro) and parsley.

Shaping dough

Make interestingly shaped loaves for a special occasion.

• Braid: cut the dough into thirds and roll these into long, thin strips. Pinch the ends of the strips together, and then braid them. Leave to rise, brush with beaten egg and sprinkle with poppy seeds before baking. Use milk bread for a richer dough.

• Oval loaves: cut the dough in half and shape each piece into a roll about

Basic bread dough

Mix 450g/1lb strong plain white bread flour with 1 sachet fast action easy-blend (rapid-rise) dried yeast, 5ml/1 tsp salt and 5ml/1 tsp sugar. Make a well in the middle and add 250ml/8fl oz/1 cup hand-hot water and 30ml/2 tbsp olive oil. Gradually work the liquid into the flour to make a stiff dough. Turn the dough out on to a lightly floured surface and knead it for about 10 minutes, or until very smooth and elastic. Shape the dough as required and place on a greased baking tray. Cover with oiled clear film (plastic wrap) and leave in a warm place until doubled in size before baking. Bake large loaves at 220°C/425°F/ Gas 7 for about 40 minutes, or until well risen and browned. Bake rolls at the same temperature for 20–25 minutes. Turn the bread over and tap the base: the loaf should sound hollow. If it sounds damp and solid it is not properly cooked through so return it to the oven for a further 5 minutes and check again.

20cm/8in long. Leave to rise, then use a sharp knife to cut shallow diagonal slits across the top before brushing with a little warm water and baking.

• Rolls: cut the dough into 12 equal portions and shape these into round or oval rolls. To make a knot, roll a portion into a thin strip and twist it into a knot. For twists, divide each portion in half, roll into strips and twist these together. Transfer the rolls to a greased baking tray and leave to rise. Brush with beaten egg or milk, then sprinkle with sesame or poppy seeds before baking.

• Swirl: make up two batches of dough: one plain white and one

Above *Warm, fresh home-baked bread can be a real feature at parties.*

seeded half and half wholemeal and white. Cut each type in half. Roll out a portion of white into an oval, and then roll a portion of seeded into a equal-size oval. Lay the seeded dough on the white and roll up both into an oval loaf. Repeat with the remaining dough to make a second loaf. Leave to rise, brush with warm water and sprinkle with seeds before baking.

Buying guide
Buy bread on the day it is to be eaten or buy and freeze it in advance, then thaw it early on the day or overnight.
• Crusty breads, such as baguettes, French and Italian country breads, and the British bloomer, are good for mopping up dressings and sauces, and they go well with cheese. Cut them into chunks to make crusty croûtons.
• Rich breads, such as milk bread, brioche or challah/cholla, are a good choice for brunch or to accompany marinated vegetables and salads for lunch. They are excellent for picnics.
• Flat breads, such as pitta, naan or soft wheat tortillas, can be used more widely than in their traditional roles. They go well with dips or pâtés, and are good filled or topped with salads, roasted vegetables, grilled or cured meat.

• Individual breads are perfect for buffets, picnics, breakfast or brunch. Croissants, bagels, English muffins and crumpets, teacakes or currant buns are real treat breads, as good packed with fabulous fillings as they are served in traditional style.
• Close-textured or coarse breads bring out the best in smoked fish, seafood, cured meats, fine pâtés and cheese. While firm dark or light rye bread can be thinly sliced, the coarser grainy breads tend to be more crumbly and are good served in thick chunks.

Serving bread
Warm bread has a better flavour and texture than cold.
• Present a whole loaf on a cutting board, with knife. For a large party, when guests are less likely to slice their own bread, the loaf may be part or completely sliced and presented with the slices re-assembled to prevent them from drying out.
• Pile warm flat or individual breads in a linen-lined basket and fold the cloth over to keep the bread warm.
• Sliced baguette and thinly cut breads complement light first courses; chunks, wedges and hearty lengths of baguette are more filling with main dishes and substantial salads.

Hot savoury breads
Slice a baguette, bloomer or crusty French country bread ring, leaving the slices attached at the base. Spread one of the following fillings on the slices and press them back together. Spread a little extra filling over the top. Wrap the loaf in foil and heat in the oven at 200°C/400°F/Gas 6 for about 15 minutes. Serve hot.
• Garlic butter: cream 115g/4oz/½ cup butter with 1 crushed garlic clove.
• Herb butter: cream 60ml/4 tbsp chopped fresh herbs into 115g/4oz/½ cup butter.

Above *Serve garlic or herby buttered baguettes warm and with napkins.*

• Anchovy and olive butter: finely chop a 50g/2oz can anchovies in olive oil, and cream with 115g/4oz/½ cup butter, gradually working in the oil from the can. Add 115g/4oz chopped black olives, a squeeze of lemon juice and freshly ground black pepper.
• Spring onion, lime and coriander butter: finely chop 4 spring onions (scallions) and a good handful of fresh coriander leaves, then cream with 115g/4oz/½ cup butter, adding the grated rind of 1 lime and a squeeze of lime juice. Add a chopped garlic clove, if you like.

Croûtons and croûtes
These can be cut into small cubes or chunks to match any dishes. Sauté them in olive oil and butter or bake until crisp and lightly browned, then drizzle with a little oil. Alternatively, lightly brush slices of bread with oil and grill (broil) until golden, then cut into cubes.
• Croûtes are bread slices, brushed with melted butter or oil, and baked, grilled or fried until golden on both sides. They may be small and thin, or thick and crusty slices. Croûtes complement soft foods or make a good base to absorb juices.

welcome
nibbles

Stylish snacks and little bites set every gathering
off to the right start. Choose a variety of different tastes
and textures to complement the drinks you serve.

Tortilla Chips

A useful and quick-to-prepare appetizer, tortilla chips or totopos as they are also known are excellent for scooping up a salsa or dip. They can also be sprinkled with a little grated cheese and grilled until golden, then served with a selection of other nibbles. Use corn tortillas that are a few days old; fresh tortillas will not crisp up so well.

Makes 48

8 corn tortillas
oil, for frying
salt

COOK'S TIP

The oil needs to be very hot for cooking the tortillas chips – test it first by carefully adding one of the wedges to the frying pan. It should float and begin to bubble in the oil immediately.

1 Cut each corn tortilla into six triangular wedges. Pour oil into a large, heavy bottomed frying pan to a depth of 1cm/½ in, place the pan over a medium heat and heat until very hot (see Cook's Tip).

VARIATION

To give a spicy flavour to the chips, prepare a mixture of garlic salt, paprika and a pinch of mace. Sprinkle over the freshly drained tortilla chips while they are still hot.

2 Fry the tortilla wedges in the hot oil in small batches until they turn golden and are crisp. This will only take a few moments. Remove with a slotted spoon and drain on kitchen paper. Sprinkle with salt.

3 The tortillas should be served warm. They can be cooled completely and stored in an airtight container for a few days, but will need to be reheated in a microwave or a warm oven before being served.

Pepitas

These crunchy, spicy and slightly sweet pumpkin seeds are absolutely irresistible, especially if you use hot and tasty chipotle chillies to spice them up. Their smoky flavour is the perfect foil for the nutty taste of the pumpkin seeds and the hint of sweetness provided by the sugar. Serve pepitas with pre-dinner drinks and cocktails as an alternative to nuts.

Makes 2 bowls

250g/9oz/2 cups pumpkin seeds
8 garlic cloves, crushed
2.5ml/½ tsp salt
20ml/4 tsp crushed dried chillies
10ml/2 tsp caster (superfine) sugar
2 wedges of lime

1 Heat a small, heavy frying pan, add the pumpkin seeds and dry fry for a few minutes, stirring constantly as they swell.

COOK'S TIPS

• It is important to keep the pumpkin seeds moving as they cook. Watch them carefully and do not let them burn, or they will taste bitter.
• Chipotle chillies are smoke-dried jalapeño chillies.

2 When all the seeds have swollen, add the garlic and cook for a few minutes more, stirring constantly. Add the salt and the crushed chillies and stir to mix. Turn off the heat, but keep the pan on the stove. Sprinkle the sugar over the seeds and shake the pan to ensure that they are all coated.

3 Tip the pepitas into a bowl and serve with the wedge of lime for squeezing over the seeds. If the lime is omitted, the seeds can be cooled and stored in an airtight container for serving cold or reheating later, but they are best served fresh and warm.

VARIATION

If you are using the pepitas cold, they can be mixed with cashew nuts and dried cranberries to make a spicy and fruity bowl of nibbles.

Salmon and Trout Canapés

These tiny little bites are ideal for serving with a glass of chilled sparkling wine or as part of a finger buffet.

Serves 10 to 12

For the salmon and dill squares
15ml/1 tbsp olive oil
175g/6oz salmon fillet, skinned
500g/1¼lb sliced pumpernickel bread
mayonnaise, for spreading
1 small cucumber, thinly sliced
60ml/4 tbsp sour cream
30ml/2 tbsp chopped fresh dill
10ml/2 tsp lemon juice
½ red (bell) pepper, seeded and
*   finely chopped*
salt and ground black pepper

For the smoked trout squares
5 thin slices white bread, toasted
75g/3oz/scant ½ cup cream cheese
*   with garlic and herbs*
75g/3oz smoked trout, skinned
finely grated rind of 2 lemons
lemon wedges, to garnish

1 Heat the oil in a griddle pan. Season the salmon fillet well on both sides and fry for 5–8 minutes or until the flesh is opaque. Remove from the pan and leave to cool.

2 Using a fluted 5cm/2in cutter, cut out 24 squares from the sliced pumpernickel. Spread a little mayonnaise on each bread square and top with a cucumber slice.

3 Flake the salmon into bitesize pieces and remove any remaining bones.

4 Put the fish in a bowl and mix with the sour cream, dill and lemon juice. Season with salt and ground black pepper to taste.

5 Spread a little of the mixture on each pumpernickel square and top with pieces of red pepper.

6 Make the smoked trout squares. Trim the crusts from the toast and spread a fifth of the cream cheese on each slice. Cut each slice into four squares.

7 Cut the smoked trout into pieces and divide among the toast squares. Sprinkle the lemon rind over the trout and season with plenty of pepper.

8 Arrange the canapés on a large serving platter or separate plates and garnish with the lemon wedges. Chill until ready to serve.

VARIATION
To make cream cheese and salmon canapes, cut a small French stick into thin slices. Spread each slice with a little cream cheese, then top with smoked salmon and a sprig of fresh dill. Serve with lemon wedges for squeezing over.

Spicy Potato Wedges with Chilli Dip

These dry-roasted potato wedges with crisp spicy crusts are delicious with the chilli dip. They make a tasty appetizer or can be served with other dishes as part of a barbecue or informal buffet supper.

Serves 6

4 baking potatoes, about 225g/
  8oz each
60ml/4 tbsp olive oil
4 garlic cloves, crushed
10ml/2 tsp ground allspice
10ml/2 tsp ground coriander
30ml/2 tbsp paprika
salt and ground black pepper

For the dip

30ml/2 tbsp olive oil
2 small onions, finely chopped
2 garlic clove, crushed
400g/14oz can chopped tomatoes
2 fresh red chillies, seeded and
  finely chopped
30ml/2 tbsp balsamic vinegar
30ml/2 tbsp chopped fresh coriander
  (cilantro), plus extra to garnish

1 Preheat the oven to 200°C/400°F/ Gas 6. Cut the potatoes in half, then into eight wedges.

2 Add the wedges to a large pan of cold water. Bring to the boil, reduce the heat and simmer for 10 minutes or until the wedges have softened but the flesh has not started to disintegrate. Drain well and pat dry on kitchen paper.

3 Mix the olive oil, garlic, allspice, coriander and paprika in a roasting pan. Add salt and pepper to taste. Add the potatoes to the pan and shake to coat them thoroughly. Roast for 20–25 minutes, until the wedges are browned, crisp and fully cooked. Turn the potato wedges occasionally during the roasting time.

4 Meanwhile, make the chilli dip. Heat the oil in a small pan, add the onion and garlic, and cook for 5–10 minutes until soft.

5 Tip in the chopped tomatoes, with any juice. Stir in the chilli and vinegar. Cook gently for 10 minutes until the mixture has reduced and thickened, then taste and check the seasoning. Stir in the chopped fresh coriander.

6 Pile the spicy potato wedges on a plate, garnish with the extra coriander and serve with the chilli dip.

VARIATION
Instead of balsamic vinegar, try brown rice vinegar, which has a mellow flavour.

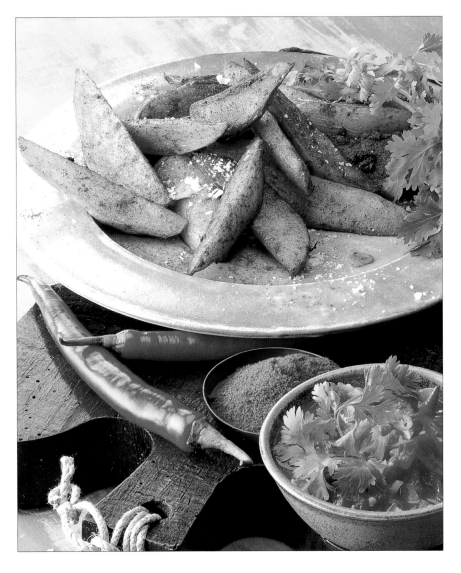

Party Eggs

Hard-boiled eggs make perfect party food. Use a variety of fillings for a stunning centrepiece. Double the quantities if you are making larger batches.

Each variation fills 6 eggs

EGGS WITH CAVIAR

6 eggs, hard-boiled
4 spring onions (scallions), trimmed
  and very finely sliced
30ml/2 tbsp sour cream
5ml/1 tsp lemon juice
25g/1oz/2 tbsp caviar
salt and ground black pepper
lemon rind and caviar, to garnish

Mix all the ingredients with the egg yolks, spoon back into the egg whites and garnish with lemon rind and caviar.

PRAWN AND CUCUMBER EGGS

6 eggs, hard-boiled
75g/3oz/scant 1 cup cooked peeled
  prawns (shrimp), reserving 12 for
  garnish and the rest chopped
25g/1oz cucumber, peeled and diced
5ml/1 tsp tomato ketchup
15ml/1 tbsp lemon mayonnaise
salt and ground black pepper
fennel sprigs, to garnish

Mix all the ingredients with the egg yolks, spoon back into the egg whites and garnish with prawns and fennel.

NUTTY DEVILLED EGGS

6 eggs, hard-boiled
40g/1½oz cooked ham, chopped
4 walnut halves, very finely chopped
15ml/1 tbsp Dijon mustard
15ml/1 tbsp mayonnaise
5ml/1 tsp white wine vinegar
few large pinches of cayenne pepper
salt and ground black pepper
paprika and gherkins, to garnish

Mix together all the ingredients with the egg yolks, spoon into the whites and garnish with paprika and gherkin slices.

GARLIC AND GREEN PEPPERCORN EGGS

5ml/1 tsp garlic purée or 1 large garlic
  clove, crushed
45ml/3 tbsp crème fraîche
6 eggs, hard-boiled
salt and ground black pepper
2.5ml/½ tsp green peppercorns,
  crushed, to garnish

Mix the garlic, crème fraîche, egg yolks and seasoning. Place in a piping bag and pipe into the egg whites. Sprinkle with a few crushed peppercorns.

Bitesize Cheese Brioches

These mouthfuls of golden, buttery dough have a surprise in the middle: a nugget of melting cheese, so be sure to serve them warm to enjoy them at their best.

Makes about 40

450g/1lb/4 cups plain (all-purpose) or
    strong white bread flour, plus extra
    for dusting
5ml/1 tsp salt
5ml/1 tsp ground turmeric
1 sachet easy-blend (rapid-rise)
    dried yeast
150ml/¼ pint/⅔ cup warm milk
2 eggs, plus 2 egg yolks
75g/3oz/6 tbsp butter, melted
    and slightly cooled
50g/2oz/½ cup grated Cheddar cheese
oil, for greasing
50g/2oz/½ cup cubed cheese, such as
    Cheshire, Gouda or Port Salut

1 Sift the dry ingredients into a large bowl with the yeast and make a hollow in the middle. Mix the milk, eggs and one yolk with the butter and Cheddar.

2 Pour the liquid into the bowl of dry ingredients and blend with a fork to bring the mixture together. Continue mixing in the bowl or in a food processor with a dough blade, until it is evenly mixed. Turn out the mixture on to a lightly floured surface and knead, working in as little flour as possible, until the surface of the mixture becomes smooth and dry.

3 Place the dough in a lightly oiled bowl. Lightly oil the top of the dough, cover with a clean cloth and leave in a warm place for at least 1 hour, until the dough has doubled in bulk.

4 Turn out on to a floured surface and knead the dough until it becomes firm and elastic again.

5 Divide the dough into four batches, then divide each batch into eight to ten pieces. Knead each piece until smooth.

COOK'S TIP

For a special party, use gold petits fours cases; they are firmer and give more support, and they look smart and elegant.

6 Press a cube of cheese into the middle of each piece of dough, then shape into a round and place in paper sweet (candy) cases. Place the paper cases in mini muffin trays to support the soft dough during baking or, alternatively, put the dough in doubled paper cases. Set the brioches aside in a warm place until they are well risen and have almost doubled in size.

7 Preheat the oven to 200°C/400°F/Gas 6. Mix the remaining yolk with 15ml/1 tbsp water and glaze the brioches with the mixture, using a pastry brush. Bake for about 15 minutes, or until golden brown, well-risen and firm underneath if tapped.

Stilton Croquettes

These are perfect little party bites, which you can make in advance and reheat at the last minute. For a really crisp result, double coat the croquettes in breadcrumbs.

Makes about 20

350g/12oz floury potatoes, cooked
75g/3oz/¾ cup creamy Stilton
*   cheese, crumbled*
3 eggs, hard-boiled, peeled
*   and chopped*
few drops of Worcestershire sauce
plain (all-purpose) flour, for coating
1 egg, beaten
45–60ml/3–4 tbsp fine, dry
*   breadcrumbs*
vegetable oil, for deep-frying
salt and ground black pepper
dipping sauce or salsa, to serve

1 Mash the potatoes until they are quite smooth. Work in the crumbled Stilton cheese, chopped egg and Worcestershire sauce. Add salt and ground black pepper to taste.

2 Divide the potato and cheese mixture into about 20 portions. Dust your hands lightly with flour and shape the pieces into small sausage shapes, no longer than 2.5cm/1in in length.

3 Coat in flour, then dip into the beaten egg and coat evenly in breadcrumbs. Reshape, if necessary. Chill for about 30 minutes then deep-fry, seven to eight at a time, in hot oil turning frequently until they are golden brown all over. Drain on kitchen paper, transfer to a serving dish and keep warm for up to 30 minutes. Serve with a dipping sauce such as soy sauce or a tomato salsa.

Cheese and Potato Bread Twists

These individual "ploughman's lunch" twists have the cheese cooked in the bread. They can be filled with smoked salmon seasoned with lemon juice after cooking to make them extra special.

Makes 12

225g/8oz potatoes, diced
225g/8oz/2 cups strong white bread
*   flour, plus extra for dusting*
5ml/1 tsp easy-blend (rapid-rise)
*   dried yeast*
150ml/¼ pint/⅔ cup lukewarm water
175g/6oz/1½ cups finely grated red
*   Leicester cheese*
10ml/2 tsp olive oil, for greasing
salt

1 Cook the potatoes in a large pan with plenty of lightly salted boiling water for 20 minutes, or until tender. Drain through a colander and return to the pan. Mash until smooth and set aside to cool.

2 Meanwhile, sift the flour into a large bowl and add the yeast and a good pinch of salt. Stir in the mashed potatoes and rub with your fingers to form a crumb consistency.

VARIATION
Any hard, well-flavoured cheese can be used. Mature (sharp) Cheddar is the traditional choice for a ploughman's lunch, or you could try a smoked cheese or a variety with added herbs.

3 Make a well in the centre of the dough and pour in the lukewarm water. Start by bringing the mixture together with a round-bladed knife then use your hands. Knead for 5 minutes on a well-floured surface. Return the dough to the bowl. Cover with a damp cloth and leave the dough to rise in a warm place for 1 hour or until doubled in size.

4 Turn the dough out and knock back (punch down) the air bubbles. Knead again for a few seconds.

5 Divide the dough into 12 even pieces and shape into rounds.

6 Sprinkle the cheese over a baking sheet. Take each ball of dough and roll it in the cheese.

7 Roll each cheese-covered roll on a dry surface to form a long sausage shape. Fold the two ends together and twist the bread. Lay the bread twists on an oiled baking sheet.

8 Cover with a damp cloth and leave the bread to rise in a warm place for 30 minutes. Preheat the oven to 220°C/425°F/Gas 7. Bake the bread for 10–15 minutes. These bread twists stay moist and fresh for up to 3 days if stored in airtight food bags.

Potato and Onion Tortilla with Broad Beans

This Spanish omelette, which includes herbs and broad beans, is ideal for a summer party when cut into pieces and served as a tapa.

Serves 8 to 10

45ml/3 tbsp olive oil
2 Spanish onions, thinly sliced
300g/11oz waxy potatoes, cut into
*   1cm/½in dice*
250g/9oz/1½ cups shelled broad
*   (fava) beans*
5ml/1 tsp chopped fresh thyme or
*   summer savory*
6 large (US extra large) eggs
45ml/3 tbsp mixed chopped chives
*   and chopped flat leaf parsley*
salt and ground black pepper

1 Heat 30ml/2 tbsp of the oil in a 23cm/9in deep non-stick frying pan. Add the onions and potatoes and stir to coat. Cover and cook gently, stirring frequently, for 20–25 minutes, or until the potatoes are cooked and the onions collapsed. Do not let the vegetables turn brown.

2 Meanwhile, cook the beans in salted boiling water for 5 minutes. Drain well and set aside to cool.

3 When the beans are cool enough to handle, peel off the grey outer skins. Add the beans to the frying pan, together with the thyme or savory and season with salt and pepper to taste. Stir well and cook for 2–3 minutes.

4 Beat the eggs with salt and pepper to taste, add the mixed herbs, then pour over the potatoes and onions and increase the heat slightly. Cook gently until the egg on the bottom sets and browns, gently pulling the omelette away from the sides of the pan and tilting it to allow the uncooked egg to run underneath.

5 Invert the tortilla on to a plate. Add the remaining oil to the pan and heat until hot. Slip the tortilla back into the pan, uncooked side down, and cook for another 3–5 minutes to allow the underneath to brown.

6 Slide the tortilla out on to a clean plate. Use a sharp knife to cut the tortilla into eight to ten pieces or small squares and serve warm.

COOK'S TIP

Cook the tortilla very gently once the eggs have been added to the pan – trying to speed up the cooking process by raising the temperature browns the underneath much too soon, before the egg has time to set.

finger food and light bites

Standing-and-eating food has to be easy to eat and sufficiently satisfying to keep everyone munching through hours of chatting.

Prawn and Sesame Toasts

These attractive little canapés are ideal for serving with pre-dinner drinks and are always a favourite hot snack at parties. They are surprisingly easy to prepare and you can cook them in just a few minutes. Serve with chilli sauce.

Serves 4

225g/8oz peeled raw prawns (shrimp)
15ml/1 tbsp sherry
15ml/1 tbsp soy sauce
30ml/2 tbsp cornflour (cornstarch)
2 egg whites
115g/4oz/½ cup sesame seeds
4 slices white bread, each cut into
  4 triangular quarters or 4 slices
oil, for deep-frying
sweet chilli sauce, to serve

1 Process the prawns, sherry, soy sauce and cornflour in a food processor.

2 In a scrupulously grease-free bowl, whisk the egg whites until they are stiff. Fold them into the prawn and cornflour mixture.

3 Spread out the sesame seeds on a plate. Spread the prawn paste over one side of each bread triangle.

4 Press the coated sides of the bread into the sesame seeds so they stick and cover the prawn paste.

5 Heat the oil in a wok or deep-fryer, to 190°C/375°F or until a cube of bread, added to the oil, browns in about 45 seconds. Add the toasts, a few at a time, prawn side down, and deep-fry for 2–3 minutes, then turn and fry on the other side until golden. Drain.

Quesadillas

These cheese-filled tortillas are the Mexican equivalent of toasted sandwiches. Serve them hot or they will become chewy. If you are making them for a crowd, fill and fold the tortillas ahead of time, but only cook them to order.

Serves 8

400g/14oz mozzarella, Monterey Jack or mild Cheddar cheese
2 fresh fresno chillies (optional)
16 wheat flour tortillas, about 15cm/6in across
onion relish or tomato salsa, to serve

1 If using mozzarella cheese, it must be drained thoroughly and then patted dry and sliced into thin strips. Monterey Jack and Cheddar cheese should both be coarsely grated, as finely grated cheese will melt and ooze away when cooking. Set the cheese aside in a bowl.

2 If using the chillies, spear them on a long-handled metal skewer and roast them over the flame of a gas burner until the skin blisters and darkens. Do not let the flesh burn. Place the roasted chillies in a strong plastic bag and tie the top to keep the steam in. Set aside for 20 minutes for the skin to loosen.

VARIATIONS
Try spreading a thin layer of your favourite salsa on the tortillas before adding the cheese, or add some cooked chicken or prawns (shrimp) before folding the tortillas.

3 Remove the roasted chillies from the bag and carefully peel off the skin. Cut off the stalk, then slit the chillies and scrape out all the seeds. Cut the flesh into 16 even-sized thin strips.

4 Warm a large frying pan or griddle. Place one tortilla on the pan or griddle at a time, sprinkle about one sixteenth of the cheese on to one half and add a strip of chilli, if using. Fold the tortilla over the cheese and press the edges together gently to seal. Cook the filled tortilla for 1 minute, then turn over and cook the other side for 1 minute.

5 Remove the filled tortilla from the pan or griddle, cut it into three triangles or four strips and serve immediately while it still hot, with the onion relish or tomato salsa.

Mozzarella and Tomato Skewers

Stacks of flavour – layers of oven-baked mozzarella, tomatoes, basil and bread. These colourful kebabs will be popular with children and adults alike, so make plenty for everyone to enjoy.

Serves 10 to 12

24 slices white country bread, each about 1cm/½in thick
90ml/6 tbsp olive oil
250g/9oz mozzarella cheese, cut into 5mm/¼in slices
6 ripe plum tomatoes, cut into 5mm/¼in slices
25g/1oz/1 cup fresh basil leaves, plus extra to garnish
salt and ground black pepper
60ml/4 tbsp chopped fresh flat leaf parsley, to garnish

1 Preheat the oven to 220°C/425°F/ Gas 7. Trim the crusts from the bread and cut each slice into four equal squares. Arrange on baking sheets and brush with half the olive oil. Bake for 3–5 minutes until the squares are a pale golden colour.

2 Remove the bread squares from the oven and place them on a chopping board with the other ingredients.

3 Make 32 stacks, each starting with a square of bread, then a slice of the mozzarella cheese topped with a slice of tomato and a basil leaf. Sprinkle with salt and pepper, then repeat, ending with a piece of bread. Push a skewer through each stack and place on the baking sheets. Drizzle with the remaining oil and bake for 10–15 minutes until the cheese begins to melt. Garnish with basil and parsley.

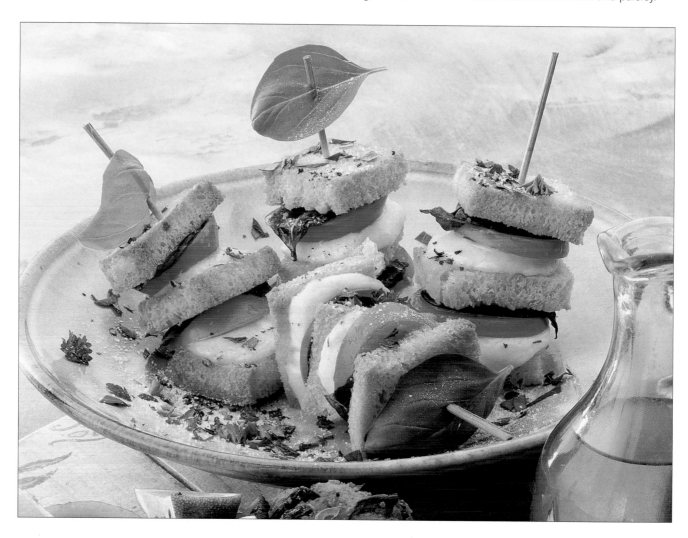

Mussels in Black Bean Sauce

The large green-shelled mussels from New Zealand are perfect for this delicious dish. Buy the cooked mussels on the half-shell – it is an elegant way to serve them.

Makes 20

15ml/1 tbsp vegetable oil
2.5cm/1in piece of fresh root ginger, finely chopped
2 garlic cloves, finely chopped
1 fresh red chilli, seeded and chopped
15ml/1 tbsp black bean sauce
15ml/1 tbsp dry sherry
5ml/1 tsp granulated sugar
5ml/1 tsp sesame oil
10ml/2 tsp dark soy sauce
20 cooked New Zealand green-shelled mussels
2 spring onions (scallions), 1 shredded and 1 cut into fine rings

1 Heat the vegetable oil in a pan or wok. Fry the ginger, garlic and chilli with the black bean sauce for a few seconds, then add the sherry and sugar and cook for 30 seconds more, stirring with cooking chopsticks or a wooden spoon to ensure the sugar is dissolved.

2 Remove from the heat, stir in the oil and soy sauce. Mix thoroughly.

COOK'S TIP
Provide cocktail sticks (toothpicks) for spearing the mussels and removing them from their half-shells.

3 Have ready a bamboo steamer or a medium pan holding 5cm/2in of simmering water, and fitted with a metal trivet. Place the mussels in layers on a heatproof plate that will fit inside the steamer or pan. Spoon the prepared sauce evenly over the half-shell mussels.

4 Sprinkle all the spring onions over the mussels. Place in the steamer or cover the plate tightly with foil and place it on the trivet in the pan. It should be just above the level of the water. Cover and steam over a high heat for about 10 minutes or until the mussels have heated through. Serve immediately.

Futo-Maki

Thick-rolled sushi, such as futo-maki, is a fashionable and attractive food to serve as canapés with drinks.

Makes 16

2 nori sheets

For the su-meshi (vinegared rice)
200g/7oz/1 cup short grain rice
275ml/9fl oz/scant 1¼ cups water
45ml/3 tbsp rice vinegar
37.5ml/7½ tsp sugar
10ml/2 tsp salt

For the omelette
2 eggs, beaten
25ml/1½ tbsp second dashi stock
10ml/2 tsp sake
2.5ml/½ tsp salt
vegetable oil, for frying

For the fillings
4 dried shiitake mushrooms,
  soaked in water overnight
120ml/4fl oz/½ cup second dashi stock
15ml/1 tbsp shoyu
7.5ml/1½ tsp sugar
5ml/1 tsp mirin
6 raw king prawns (jumbo shrimp),
  heads and shells removed
4 asparagus spears, boiled and cooled
10 chives, about 23cm/9in long
salt
wasabi, gari and soy sauce, to serve

1 To make the su-meshi, wash the rice in cold water, drain and set aside for one hour. Put the rice into a pan and add the water. Cover and boil for 5 minutes, then simmer until the water has been absorbed. Remove from the heat and set aside for 10 minutes.

2 Mix the rice vinegar with the sugar and salt. Tip the rice into a bowl and sprinkle with the vinegar mixture. Fold into the rice with a spatula, but do not stir. Cool the su-meshi before shaping.

3 For the omelette, mix the beaten eggs, dashi stock, sake and salt in a bowl. Heat a little oil in a frying pan on a medium-low heat. Pour in just enough egg mixture to cover the base of the pan. As soon as the mixture sets, fold the omelette in half towards you and wipe the space left with a little oil. With the first omelette still in the pan, repeat until all the mixture is used.

4 Each new omelette is laid on to the first to form a multi-layered omelette. Slide the layered omelette on to a chopping board. When cool, cut lengthways into 1cm/½ in wide strips.

5 Put the shiitake mushrooms and the water, stock, shoyu, sugar and mirin in a small pan. Bring to the boil, then reduce the heat to low. Cook for 20 minutes, or until half of the liquid has evaporated. Drain the shiitake mushrooms, remove and discard the stalks, and slice the caps thinly. Squeeze out any excess liquid, then dry on kitchen paper. Discard the liquid.

6 Make three cuts in the belly of each of the prawns to stop them curling up, and boil in salted water for 1 minute, or until they turn bright pink. Drain and cool, then remove the vein using a cocktail stick (toothpick).

COOK'S TIP
If you make the rolled sushi ahead, wrap each roll in clear film (plastic wrap) until ready to slice and serve the rolls.

7 Place a nori sheet, rough side up, at the front edge of a sushi rolling mat. Scoop up half of the su-meshi and spread it on the nori. Leave a 1cm/½ in margin at the side nearest you, and 2cm/¾ in at the side furthest from you. Make a shallow depression lengthways across the centre of the rice. Fill this with half the omelette strips and half the asparagus. Place half the prawns along the egg and asparagus. Top with five chives and half the shiitake slices.

8 Lift the mat with your thumbs while pressing the filling with your fingers. Roll the mat up gently. When completed, gently roll the mat to firm it up. Unwrap and set the futo-maki aside. Repeat to make another roll.

9 Cut each futo-maki into eight pieces, using a very sharp knife. Wipe the knife with a clean dishtowel dampened with rice vinegar after each cut.

10 Line up all the pieces on a large tray or serving platter. Serve with small dishes of wasabi, gari and soy sauce for dipping.

Crab Egg Rolls

These wonderful crab rolls are similar to authentic Chinese spring rolls. They are made with wafer-thin pancakes, which provide the very crisp case for the filling. If you prefer a softer version the rolls can be steamed – they are equally delicious and quite light. These are ideal for buffets, children's parties and summer picnics.

Makes about 12

3 eggs
450ml/¾ pint/scant 2 cups water
175g/6oz/1½ cups plain
*   (all-purpose) flour*
2.5ml/½ tsp salt
oil, for deep-frying
lime wedges, to serve
45ml/3 tbsp light soy sauce mixed with
*   5ml/1 tsp sesame oil, for dipping*

For the filling
225g/8oz/1⅓ cups white crab meat
*   or small prawns (shrimp)*
3 large spring onions
*   (scallions), shredded*
2.5cm/1in piece of fresh root
*   ginger, grated*
2 large garlic cloves, chopped
115g/4oz bamboo shoots, chopped,
*   or beansprouts*
15ml/1 tbsp soy sauce
10–15ml/2–3 tsp cornflour (cornstarch)
*   blended with 15ml/1 tbsp water*
1 egg, separated
salt and ground black pepper

1 Lightly beat the eggs and gradually stir in the water. Sift the flour and salt into another bowl and work in the egg mixture. Blend to a smooth batter, then remove any lumps if necessary. Leave to rest for 20 minutes.

2 When ready to use, lightly whisk the batter and stir in 15ml/1 tbsp cold water to thin it slightly if necessary.

3 Lightly grease a 25cm/10in non-stick frying pan and heat gently. To make smooth, pale wrappers for the egg rolls, the frying pan must be hot enough to set the batter, but should not be hot enough for the batter to brown, bubble or develop holes. Pour in about 45ml/3 tbsp batter and swirl round the pan to spread evenly and very thinly. Cook for 2 minutes, or until loose underneath. There is no need to cook the pancake on the other side.

4 Make a further 11 pancakes. Stack the pancakes, cooked side upwards, between sheets of baking parchment. Set aside until ready to use.

5 To make the filling, combine the crab or prawns, spring onions, ginger, garlic, bamboo shoots or beansprouts, soy sauce, cornflour and water, egg yolk and seasoning.

6 Lightly beat the egg white. Place a spoonful of filling in the middle of each pancake, brush the edges with egg white and fold into neat parcels, tucking in the ends well.

7 Heat the oil in a deep-frying pan and when a cube of bread turns light golden in 1 minute carefully add four of the parcels, fold side downwards. Cook for 1–2 minutes, or until golden and crisp. Remove with a slotted spoon and place on kitchen paper. Keep warm in the oven while you cook the remaining egg rolls. Alternatively, using a stacking bamboo steamer, arrange four parcels in each layer, cover with a lid and steam for 30 minutes.

8 Serve with the soy sauce and sesame oil dipping sauce and wedges of lime.

Tortilla Cones with Smoked Salmon and Soft Cheese

These simple yet sophisticated wraps are a must for serving with drinks or as part of a buffet.

Makes 8

*115g/4oz/½ cup soft white
 (farmer's) cheese
30ml/2 tbsp roughly chopped fresh dill
juice of 1 lemon
1 small red onion
15ml/1 tbsp drained bottled capers
30ml/2 tbsp extra virgin olive oil
30ml/2 tbsp roughly chopped fresh flat
 leaf parsley
115g/4oz smoked salmon
8 small wheat flour tortillas
salt and ground black pepper
lemon wedges, for squeezing*

3 Cut the smoked salmon into short, thin strips and add to the red onion mixture. Toss to mix. Season to taste with plenty of pepper.

COOK'S TIP
You can use salted capers in this dish instead of the unsalted variety, but rinse them thoroughly before using.

4 Spread a little of the soft cheese mixture on each tortilla and top with the smoked salmon mixture.

5 Roll up the tortillas into cones and secure with wooden cocktail sticks (toothpicks). Arrange on a serving plate and add some lemon wedges, for squeezing. Serve immediately.

1 Place the soft cheese in a bowl and mix in half the chopped dill. Add a little salt and pepper and a dash of the lemon juice to taste. Reserve the remaining lemon juice in a separate mixing bowl.

2 Finely chop the red onion. Add the onion, capers and olive oil to the lemon juice in the mixing bowl. Add the chopped flat leaf parsley and the remaining dill and gently stir.

VARIATION
Tortilla cones can be filled with a variety of ingredients. Try soft cheese with red pesto and chopped sun-dried tomatoes, or mackerel pâté with slices of cucumber.

Tunisian Brik

You can make these little parcels into any shape you like, but the most important thing is to encase the egg white quickly before it starts to escape.

Makes 6

45ml/3 tbsp butter, melted
1 small red onion, finely chopped
150g/5oz chicken or turkey
 fillet, minced (ground)
1 large garlic clove, crushed
juice of ½ lemon
30ml/2 tbsp chopped fresh parsley
12 sheets of filo pastry, each about
 15 x 25cm/6 x 10in, thawed if frozen
6 small (US medium) eggs, such as
 bantam, pheasant or guinea fowl
oil, for deep-frying
salt and ground black pepper

1 Heat half the butter in a pan and sauté the onion for 3 minutes. Add the chicken or turkey, garlic, lemon juice, parsley and seasoning, and cook, stirring, for 2–3 minutes, or until the meat is just cooked. Set aside to cool.

COOK'S TIP
If you prefer to cook these pastries in the oven, preheat it to 220°C/425°F/Gas 7. Brush the pastries with butter or beaten egg and cook for 8–10 minutes.

2 Place one sheet of pastry lengthways on the work surface and brush with melted butter; top with a second sheet. Brush the edges with butter and place one-sixth of the mixture about 2.5cm/1in from the bottom left-hand side of the pastry sheet. Flatten the filling, making a slight hollow in it.

3 Carefully crack an egg into the hollow and fold up the pastry immediately so the egg white does not run out. Lift the right-hand edge and fold it over to the left edge to enclose the filling and seal quickly. Fold the bottom left-hand corner straight up and then fold the bottom left corner up to the right edge, forming a triangle.

4 Use the remaining pastry sheets and filling to make another five parcels, then heat the oil in a frying pan until a cube of bread turns golden in about 1½ minutes. Cook the pastries, two to three at a time, until golden. Lift them out of the pan with a slotted spoon and drain on kitchen paper. Serve hot or cold.

Mini Ham, Roasted Pepper and Mozzarella Ciabatta Pizzas

These quick ciabatta pizzas are eye-catching with their bright pepper topping and great for children.

Serves 8

2 red (bell) peppers
2 yellow (bell) peppers
1 loaf ciabatta bread
8 slices prosciutto or other thinly-sliced
  ham, cut into thick strips
150g/5oz mozzarella cheese
ground black pepper
tiny basil leaves, to garnish

1 Preheat a grill (broiler), Grill the peppers, skin sides uppermost, until they are black. Place them in a bowl, cover and leave for 10 minutes. Peel off the skins.

2 Cut the bread into eight thick slices and toast both sides until golden.

3 Cut the roasted peppers into thick strips and arrange them on the toasted bread with the strips of prosciutto or other ham.

4 Thinly slice the mozzarella cheese and arrange on top. Grind over plenty of black pepper. Place under a hot grill for 2–3 minutes until the cheese is bubbling.

5 Arrange the fresh basil leaves on top and to serve transfer to a serving dish or platter. Allow the cheese to cool for a few minutes, if serving the mini-pizzas to children.

Prosciutto and Mozzarella Parcels on Frisée Salad

Italian prosciutto crudo is a delicious raw smoked ham. Here it is baked with melting mozzarella in a light, crisp pastry case, making it an ideal finger food or as a first course with a fresh frisée salad.

Serves 6

a little hot chilli sauce
6 prosciutto crudo slices
200g/7oz mozzarella cheese, cut into
  6 slices
6 sheets filo pastry, each measuring
  45 x 28cm/18 x 11in, thawed if frozen
50g/2oz/¼ cup butter, melted
150g/5oz frisée lettuce, to serve

1 Preheat the oven to 200°C/400°F/ Gas 6. Sprinkle a little of the chilli sauce over each slice of prosciutto crudo. Place a slice of mozzarella on each slice of prosciutto, then fold it around the cheese. The cheese should be enclosed by the ham.

2 Brush a sheet of filo pastry with melted butter and fold it in half to give a double-thick piece measuring 23 x 14cm/9 x 5½in. Place a prosciutto and mozzarella parcel in the middle of the pastry and brush the remaining pastry with a little butter, then fold it over to enclose the prosciutto and mozzarella in a neat parcel. Place on a baking sheet with the edges of the pastry underneath and brush with a little butter. Repeat with the remaining parcels and sheets.

3 Bake the filo parcels for 15 minutes, or until the pastry is crisp and evenly golden. Arrange the salad on six plates and add the parcels. Serve immediately.

Smoked Chicken with Peach Mayonnaise in Filo Tartlets

These tartlets require the minimum of culinary effort because smoked chicken is widely available ready cooked. The filling can be prepared a day in advance and chilled overnight but do not fill the pastry cases until you are ready to serve them or they will become soggy.

Makes 12

25g/1oz/2 tbsp butter, melted
3 sheets filo pastry, each measuring
  45 x 28cm/18 x 11in, thawed if frozen
2 skinless cooked smoked chicken
  breast fillets, finely sliced
150ml/¼ pint/⅔ cup mayonnaise
grated rind of 1 lime
30ml/2 tbsp lime juice
2 ripe peaches, peeled, stoned (pitted)
  and chopped
salt and ground black pepper
fresh tarragon sprigs, lime slices and
  salad leaves, to garnish

1 Preheat the oven to 200°C/400°F/ Gas 6. Brush 12 small individual tartlet tins (muffin pans) with a little of the melted butter. Cut each sheet of filo pastry into 12 equal rounds large enough to line the tins, allowing just enough to stand up above the tops of the tins.

2 Place a round of pastry in each tin and brush with a little butter, then add another round of pastry. Brush each with more butter and add a third round of pastry.

COOK'S TIP
To peel peaches, place them in a bowl and pour in freshly boiled water to cover. Leave to stand for 30–60 seconds (the riper the peaches, the quicker their skins loosen). Use a slotted spoon to remove 1 peach from the water. Working quickly, slit the skin with the point of a knife then slip it off. Repeat with the remaining peaches.

3 Bake the tartlets for 5 minutes, or until the pastry is golden brown. Leave in the tins for a few moments before transferring to a wire rack to cool.

4 In a mixing bowl combine the chicken, mayonnaise, lime rind and juice, peaches and salt and pepper. Chill the mixture for at least 30 minutes, or up to 12 hours overnight. When you are ready to serve the tartlets, spoon the chicken mixture into the filo tartlets. Garnish with the fresh tarragon sprigs, lime slices and salad leaves.

dips and dippers

Smooth or slightly chunky, luscious or refreshing, dips and dippers are ideal for large gatherings or instead of a formal appetizer for supper with friends.

Walnut and Garlic Dip, Salsa Verde and Yogurt with Garlic, Cucumber and Mint

Full-flavoured classic sauces and salsas make terrific dips.

WALNUT AND GARLIC DIP

Serves 4

2 x 1cm/½ in slices white bread
60ml/4 tbsp milk
150g/5oz/1¼ cups shelled walnuts
4 garlic cloves, chopped
120ml/4fl oz/½ cup mild olive oil
15–30ml/1–2 tbsp walnut oil
   (optional)
juice of 1 lemon
salt and ground black pepper
walnut or olive oil, for drizzling
paprika, for dusting (optional)

1 Remove the crusts of the white bread, and soak the slices in the milk for 5 minutes, then process with the walnuts and chopped garlic in a food processor or blender, to make a rough paste.

2 Gradually add the olive oil to the paste with the motor still running, until the mixture forms a smooth thick sauce. Blend in the walnut oil, if using.

3 Scoop the sauce into a bowl and add lemon juice to taste, season with salt and pepper and beat well.

4 Transfer to a serving bowl, drizzle over a little more walnut or olive oil, then dust lightly with paprika, if using.

SALSA VERDE

Serves 4

1–2 garlic cloves, finely chopped
25g/1oz/1 cup flat leaf parsley leaves
15g/½oz/½ cup fresh basil, mint
   or coriander (cilantro) or a mixture
   of fresh herbs
15ml/1 tbsp chopped chives
15ml/1 tbsp salted capers, rinsed
5 anchovy fillets in olive oil, drained
   and rinsed
10ml/2 tsp French mustard (tarragon or
   fines herbes mustard are both good)
120ml/4fl oz/½ cup extra virgin olive oil
grated lemon rind and juice (optional)
ground black pepper

1 Process the garlic, parsley, basil, mint or coriander, chives, capers, anchovies, mustard and 15ml/1 tbsp of the oil in a blender or food processor.

2 Gradually add the remaining oil in a thin stream with the motor running.

3 Transfer to a bowl and adjust the seasoning to taste – there should be enough salt from the capers and anchovies. Add a little lemon juice and rind if you like. Serve immediately.

VARIATIONS
Substitute fresh chervil, tarragon, dill or fennel, for the basil, mint or coriander to make a dip for prawns (shrimp).

YOGURT WITH GARLIC, CUCUMBER AND MINT

Serves 4

15cm/6in piece cucumber
5ml/1 tsp sea salt
300ml/½ pint/1¼ cups Greek
   (US strained plain) yogurt
3–4 garlic cloves, crushed
45ml/3 tbsp chopped fresh mint
ground black pepper
chopped fresh mint and/or ground
   toasted cumin seeds, to garnish

1 Slice, chop or grate the cucumber, place in a sieve and sprinkle with half the salt. Leave over a deep plate for 30 minutes to drip.

2 Rinse the cucumber in cold water, pat dry and mix with the yogurt, garlic and mint. Season to taste. Leave for 30 minutes, stir and sprinkle with fresh mint and/or toasted cumin seeds.

COOK'S TIP
To make a yogurt and garlic dressing, spoon 150ml/¼ pint/⅔ cup Greek yogurt into a bowl. Beat in 1 chopped garlic clove, 5ml/ 1 tsp French mustard and a pinch of sugar. Season. Beat in 15–30ml/1–2 tbsp olive oil and 15–30ml/1–2 tbsp chopped herbs.

Right, from top to bottom:
Walnut and Garlic Dip, Yogurt with Garlic, Cucumber and Mint, and Salsa Verde.

Avocado Salsa

A popular chunky dip that is
excellent with tortilla chips.

Makes 1 bowl

2 large ripe avocados
1 small red onion, very finely chopped
1 red or green chilli, seeded and very
    finely chopped
½–1 garlic clove, crushed (optional)
finely shredded rind of ½ lime and
    juice of 1–1½ limes
pinch of caster (superfine) sugar
225g/8oz tomatoes, seeded
    and chopped
30ml/2 tbsp roughly chopped fresh
    coriander (cilantro)
2.5–5ml/½–1 tsp ground cumin seeds
15ml/1 tbsp olive oil
15–30ml/1–2 tbsp sour cream (optional)
salt and ground black pepper
lime wedges dipped in sea salt, and
    fresh coriander sprigs, to garnish

1 Halve, stone (pit) and peel the
avocados. Set half the flesh aside and
roughly mash the remainder in a bowl
using a fork.

COOK'S TIPS
• Leaving some of the avocado in chunks
adds a slightly different texture, but if you
prefer a smoother salsa, mash all the
avocado together.
• Hard avocados will soften in a few
seconds in a microwave. Check frequently
until you get the softness that you like.

2 Add the onion, chilli, garlic (if using),
lime rind, juice of 1 lime, sugar,
tomatoes and coriander. Add the
ground cumin, seasoning and more
lime juice to taste. Stir in the olive oil.

3 Dice the remaining avocado and stir
into the avocado salsa, then cover and
leave to stand for 15 minutes so that
the flavour develops. Stir in the sour
cream, if using. Serve immediately with
lime wedges dipped in sea salt, and
fresh coriander sprigs.

Aubergine and Lemon Dip

Here is a delicious velvet-textured dish that can either be eaten as a dip with pieces of warm pitta bread, breadsticks or tortilla corn chips, or spread on slices of bread.

Makes 1 bowl

1 large aubergine (eggplant)
1 small onion, finely chopped
2 garlic cloves, finely chopped
30ml/2 tbsp olive oil
45ml/3 tbsp chopped fresh parsley
75ml/5 tbsp crème fraîche
Tabasco sauce, to taste
juice of 1 lemon, to taste
salt and ground black pepper
toast or crusty white bread, to serve

1 Preheat the grill (broiler). Place the whole aubergine on a baking sheet and grill it for 20–30 minutes, turning occasionally, until the skin is blackened and wrinkled, and the aubergine feels soft when pressed with a fork.

2 Cover the aubergine with a clean dishtowel and then set it aside to cool for 5 minutes.

3 Heat the olive oil in a frying pan and cook the finely chopped onion and garlic for 5 minutes, or until softened but not browned.

COOK'S TIP
The aubergine can also be roasted in the oven at 200°C/400°F/Gas 6 for 20 minutes.

4 Peel the skin from the aubergine. Mash the flesh into a pulpy purée.

5 Stir in the onion mixture, parsley and crème fraîche. Add the Tabasco sauce, lemon juice and seasoning to taste. Serve on toast or crusty white bread or as a dip if you prefer.

Taramasalata

This delicious smoked mullet roe speciality is perhaps one of the most famous Greek dips. It is ideal for a buffet table, or for handing round with drinks. Fingers of warm pitta bread, breadsticks or crispy crackers all make excellent dippers.

Makes 1 bowl

115g/4oz smoked mullet roe
2 garlic cloves, crushed
30ml/2 tbsp grated onion
60ml/4 tbsp olive oil
4 slices white bread, crusts removed
juice of 2 lemons
30ml/2 tbsp milk or water
ground black pepper
warm pitta bread, breadsticks or
*   crackers, to serve*

1 Place the smoked roe, garlic, onion, oil, bread and lemon juice in a blender or food processor and process briefly until just smooth.

COOK'S TIP
Since the roe of grey mullet is expensive, smoked cod's roe is often used instead for this dish. It is paler than the burnt-orange colour of mullet roe but is still very good.

2 Add the milk or water and process again for a few seconds. (This will give the taramasalata a creamier texture.)

3 Pour the taramasalata into a serving bowl, cover with clear film (plastic wrap) and chill for 1–2 hours in the refrigerator before serving. Sprinkle the dip with freshly ground black pepper just before serving.

Cheese-crusted Party Eggs

Similar to the popular Scotch egg, these whole small eggs are wrapped in a tasty herb-flavoured coating then deep-fried. Tiny bantam or quail's eggs will look dainty and are ideal for dipping into mayonnaise.

Makes 12–20

225g/8oz/4 cups stale white breadcrumbs
1 small leek, very finely chopped
225g/8oz mild but tasty cheese, grated
10ml/2 tsp garlic and herb seasoning
60ml/4 tbsp chopped fresh parsley
10ml/2 tsp mild mustard
4 eggs, separated
60–90ml/4–6 tbsp milk
12–20 small spinach or sorrel leaves, stalks removed
12 very small eggs, such as bantam, guinea fowl, or 16–20 quail's eggs, hard-boiled and peeled
50–75g/2–3oz/½–⅔ cup flour, for coating, plus extra for dusting
50g/2oz/4 tbsp sesame seeds, for coating
oil, for deep-frying
salt and ground black pepper
mayonnaise, for dipping

1 Mix the breadcrumbs, leek, cheese, seasoning, parsley and mustard. Beat together the egg yolks and milk and blend into the mixture. Whisk two egg whites until stiff and gradually work sufficient stiff egg white into the breadcrumb mixture to give a firm, dropping consistency. Chill for 1 hour.

2 Divide the mixture into 12 portions (or 16–20 if using the tiny eggs). Mould one portion in the palm of your hand, place a spinach leaf inside and then an egg and carefully shape the mixture around the egg to enclose it completely within a thin crust. Seal well and dust lightly with flour. Repeat with the remaining portions.

3 Beat the remaining egg white with 30ml/2 tbsp water, then pour into a shallow dish. Mix the flour with salt and pepper and the sesame seeds and place in another shallow dish. Dip the eggs first in the beaten egg white, then in the sesame flour. Cover and chill for at least 20 minutes.

4 Heat the oil in a pan until a crust of bread turns golden in about 1¼ minutes. Deep-fry the eggs in the hot oil, turning frequently, until they are golden brown all over. Remove the eggs with a slotted spoon, drain on kitchen paper and leave to cool completely. Serve the cooked eggs whole or sliced in half, with a bowl of good mayonnaise for dipping.

Butterfly Prawn Spiedini with Chilli and Raspberry Dip

The success of this dish depends upon the quality of the prawns that you use, so it is worthwhile getting really good ones, which have a good flavour and texture. A fruity, slightly spicy dip is such an easy, but fabulous, accompaniment.

Makes 30

30 raw king prawns (jumbo shrimp), peeled
15ml/1 tbsp sunflower oil
sea salt

For the chilli and raspberry dip
30ml/2 tbsp raspberry vinegar
15ml/1 tbsp sugar
115g/4oz/⅔ cup raspberries
1 large fresh red chilli, seeded and finely chopped

1 Soak 30 wooden skewers in cold water for 30 minutes. Make the dip by mixing the vinegar and sugar in a small pan. Heat gently until the sugar is dissolved, stirring, then add the raspberries.

2 When the raspberry juices start to flow, tip the mixture into a sieve set over a bowl. Push the raspberries through the sieve using the back of a ladle. Discard the seeds. Stir the chilli into the purée. When the dip is cold, cover and place in a cool place until it is needed.

COOK'S TIP
These mini kebabs also taste really delicious with a vibrant chilli and mango dip. Use 1 large, ripe mango in place of the raspberries.

3 Preheat the grill (broiler) or barbecue. Remove the dark spinal vein from the prawns using a small, sharp knife.

4 Make an incision down the curved back and butterfly each prawn.

5 Mix the sunflower oil with a little sea salt in a bowl. Add the prawns and toss to coat them completely.

6 Thread the prawns on to the drained skewers, spearing them head first.

7 Grill (broil) the prawns for about 5 minutes, depending on their size, turning them over once. Serve hot, with the chilli and raspberry dip.

VARIATIONS
• Thin strips of chicken breast or turkey escalope (scallop) can be seasoned and threaded on to the skewers and grilled (broiled) instead of the prawns. They are delicious with the fruity dip.
• For a vegetarian version, grill chunks of halloumi cheese or firm tofu.

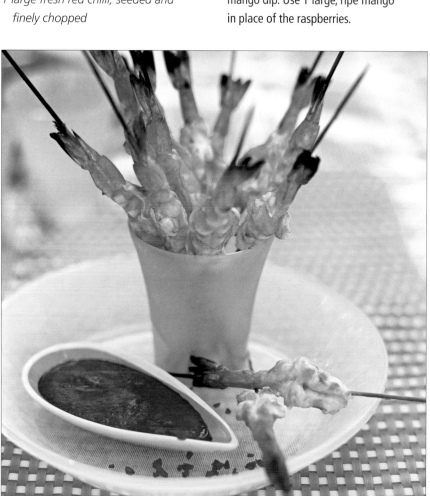

Crisp-fried Crab Claws

Crab claws are readily available in the freezer cabinet in many Asian stores and supermarkets. Thaw out thoroughly and dry on kitchen paper before dipping in the batter. They are just the right size to munch on for a burst of flavour.

Makes 12

50g/2oz/½ cup rice flour
15ml/1 tbsp cornflour (cornstarch)
2.5ml/½ tsp sugar
1 egg
60ml/4 tbsp cold water
1 lemon grass stalk, root trimmed
2 garlic cloves, finely chopped
15ml/1 tbsp chopped fresh coriander (cilantro)
1–2 fresh red chillies, seeded and finely chopped
5ml/1 tsp fish sauce (nam pla)
vegetable oil, for frying
12 half-shelled crab claws
ground black pepper

For the chilli vinegar dip
45ml/3 tbsp sugar
120ml/4fl oz/½ cup water
120ml/4fl oz/½ cup red wine vinegar
15ml/1 tbsp fish sauce
2–4 fresh red chillies, seeded and chopped

1 Combine the rice flour, cornflour and sugar in a bowl. Beat the egg with the cold water, then stir the egg and water mixture into the flour mixture and mix well until it forms a light batter.

2 Cut off the lower 5cm/2in of the lemon grass stalk and chop it finely. Add the lemon grass to the batter, with the garlic, coriander, red chillies and fish sauce. Stir in pepper to taste.

3 Make the chilli dip. Mix the sugar and water in a pan, stirring until the sugar has dissolved, then bring to the boil. Lower the heat and simmer for 5–7 minutes. Stir in the rest of the ingredients and set aside.

4 Heat the vegetable oil in a wok or deep-fryer. Pat the crab claws dry and dip into the batter. Drop the battered claws into the hot oil, a few at a time. Fry until golden brown. Drain on kitchen paper and keep hot. Pour the chilli vinegar dip into a serving bowl and serve with the hot crab claws.

VARIATION
This Asian-style batter can also be used to coat king prawns (jumbo shrimp).

Seafood Spring Onion Skewers with **Tartare Sauce**

Make these skewers quite small to serve as a canapé at a drinks party or before dinner, with the tartare sauce offered as a dip.

Makes 9

675g/1½lb monkfish, filleted, skinned and membrane removed
1 bunch thick spring onions (scallions)
75ml/5 tbsp olive oil
1 garlic clove, finely chopped
15ml/1 tbsp lemon juice
5ml/1 tsp dried oregano
30ml/2 tbsp chopped fresh flat leaf parsley
12–18 small scallops or raw king prawns (jumbo shrimp)
75g/3oz/1½ cups fine fresh breadcrumbs
salt and ground black pepper

For the tartare sauce
2 egg yolks
300ml/½ pint/1¼ cups olive oil, or vegetable oil and olive oil mixed
15–30ml/1–2 tbsp lemon juice
5ml/1 tsp French mustard, preferably tarragon mustard
15ml/1 tbsp chopped gherkin or pickled cucumber
15ml/1 tbsp chopped capers
30ml/2 tbsp chopped fresh flat leaf parsley
30ml/2 tbsp chopped fresh chives
5ml/1 tsp chopped fresh tarragon

1 Soak nine wooden skewers in water for 30 minutes to prevent them from scorching under the grill (broiler).

2 To make the tartare sauce, whisk the egg yolks and a pinch of salt. Whisk in the oil, a drop at a time at first. When about half the oil is incorporated, add it in a thin stream, whisking constantly. Stop when the mayonnaise is thick.

3 Whisk in 15ml/1 tbsp lemon juice, then a little more oil. Stir in all the mustard, gherkin or cucumber, capers, parsley, chives and tarragon. Add more lemon juice and seasoning to taste.

4 Cut the monkfish into 18 pieces; cut the spring onions into 18 pieces about 5cm/2in long. In a bowl, mix the oil, garlic, lemon juice, oregano and half the parsley with seasoning. Add the seafood and the spring onions, then marinate for 15 minutes.

5 Mix the breadcrumbs and remaining parsley together. Toss the seafood and spring onions in the mixture to coat.

6 Preheat the grill. Drain the wooden skewers and thread the monkfish, scallops or prawns and spring onions on to them. Drizzle with a little marinade then grill (broil) for 5–6 minutes in total, turning once and drizzling with the marinade, until the fish is just cooked. Serve immediately with the tartare sauce.

Stilton-stuffed Mushrooms Baked with Garlic Breadcrumbs

Serve these succulent stuffed mushrooms with warm bread.

Serves 8

900g/2lb chestnut mushrooms
6 garlic cloves, finely chopped
200g/7oz/scant 1 cup butter, melted
juice of 1 lemon
225g/8oz/2 cups Stilton cheese,
  crumbled
115g/4oz/1 cup walnuts, chopped
200g/7oz/3 cups white breadcrumbs
50g/2oz/²⁄₃ cup Parmesan cheese
60ml/4 tbsp chopped fresh parsley
salt and ground black pepper

For the sauce
225g/8oz/1 cup fromage frais or
  Greek (US strained plain) yogurt
1 bunch chopped fresh herbs
15ml/1 tbsp Dijon mustard

1 Preheat the oven to 200°C/400°F/ Gas 6. Place the mushrooms in an ovenproof dish and sprinkle half the garlic over them. Drizzle with 50g/ 2oz/¼ cup of the butter and the lemon juice. Season with salt and ground black pepper, and bake for 15–20 minutes. Leave to cool.

2 Cream the crumbled Stilton with the chopped walnuts and mix in 30ml/2 tbsp of the breadcrumbs.

3 Divide the Stilton mixture among the chestnut mushrooms.

4 To make the sauce, mix the fromage frais or Greek yogurt with the chopped fresh herbs and the Dijon mustard until thoroughly combined.

5 Preheat the grill (broiler). Mix the remaining garlic, breadcrumbs and melted butter together. Grate the Parmesan. Stir in the cheese and chopped, fresh parsley and season with plenty of ground black pepper. Cover the mushrooms with the breadcrumb mixture and grill for about 5 minutes, or until crisp and browned. Serve immediately with the sauce.

VARIATION
Use other types of mushrooms such as large flat mushrooms or ceps.

Nonya Pork Satay

These skewers of tender pork with a spicy nut coating make tasty snacks for a drinks party.

Makes 8 to 12

450g/1lb pork fillet
15ml/1 tbsp light muscovado (brown) sugar
1cm/½in cube shrimp paste
1–2 lemon grass stalks
30ml/2 tbsp coriander seeds, dry-fried
6 macadamia nuts or blanched almonds
2 onions, roughly chopped
3–6 fresh red chillies, seeded and roughly chopped
2.5ml/½ tsp ground turmeric
300ml/½ pint/1¼ cups canned coconut milk
30ml/2 tbsp groundnut (peanut) oil or sunflower oil
salt

1 Soak 8–12 bamboo skewers in water for at least 30 minutes to prevent them scorching when they are placed under the grill (broiler).

2 Cut the pork into small, bitesize chunks, then spread it out in a single layer in a shallow dish. Sprinkle with the sugar, to help release the juices, and set aside.

3 Fry the shrimp paste briefly in a foil parcel in a dry frying pan. Alternatively, warm the foil parcel on a skewer held over the gas flame.

COOK'S TIP
Nonya Pork Satay can be served either as part of a buffet or as a light party snack – in which case serve it with cubes of cooling cucumber, which contrast well with the spicy meat.

4 Cut off the lower 5cm/2in of the lemon grass stalks and chop finely. Process the dry-fried coriander seeds to a powder in a food processor. Add the nuts and chopped lemon grass, process briefly, then add the onions, chillies, shrimp paste, turmeric and a little salt; process to a fine paste.

5 Pour in the coconut milk and oil. Switch the machine on very briefly to mix. Pour the mixture over the pork and leave to marinate for 1–2 hours.

6 Preheat the grill or prepare the barbecue. Thread three or four pieces of marinated pork on to each bamboo skewer and grill (broil) or cook on the barbecue for 8–10 minutes, or until tender, basting frequently with the remaining marinade. Serve the skewers immediately while hot.

Yakitori Chicken

These Japanese-style kebabs are easy to eat and ideal for barbecues or parties.

Makes 12

6 boneless chicken thighs
1 bunch of spring onions (scallions)
shichimi (seven-flavour spice),
*   to serve (optional)*

For the yakitori sauce
150ml/¼ pint/⅔ cup Japanese
*   soy sauce*
90g/3½oz/½ cup sugar
25ml/1½ tbsp sake or dry white wine
15ml/1 tbsp plain (all-purpose) flour

1 Soak 12 wooden skewers in water for at least 30 minutes. Make the sauce. Stir the soy sauce, sugar and sake or wine into the flour in a small pan and bring to the boil, stirring. Lower the heat and simmer the mixture for 10 minutes, or until the sauce is reduced by one-third. Set aside.

2 Cut each chicken thigh into bitesize pieces and set aside.

3 Cut the spring onions into 3cm/1¼in pieces. Preheat the grill (broiler) or prepare the barbecue.

COOK'S TIP
If shichimi is difficult to obtain, paprika can be used instead.

4 Thread the chicken and spring onions alternately on to the drained skewers. Grill (broil) under a medium heat or cook on the barbecue, brushing generously several times with the sauce. Allow 5–10 minutes, or until the chicken is cooked but still moist.

5 Serve with yakitori sauce, offering shichimi with the kebabs if available.

VARIATION
Bitesize chunks of turkey breast, lean boneless pork or lamb fillet can be used instead of chicken. Small, whole button (white) mushrooms are also delicious for a vegetarian alternative.

buffet
centrepieces

These impressive buffet dishes will stand out
among salads and accompaniments. They are fuss-free
for self-service and delicious to eat.

Potato and Leek Filo Pie

This filo pastry pie filled with a wonderful mixture of potatoes, leeks, cheese, cream and herbs, makes an attractive and unusual centrepiece for a vegetarian buffet. Serve it cold, together with a choice of different salads.

Serves 8

800g/1¾ lb new potatoes, sliced
400g/14oz leeks (trimmed weight)
75g/3oz/6 tbsp butter
15g/½ oz/¼ cup finely chopped
    fresh parsley
60ml/4 tbsp chopped mixed fresh
    herbs, such as chervil, chives,
    a little tarragon and basil
12 sheets filo pastry, thawed if frozen
150g/5oz white Cheshire, Lancashire
    or Sonoma Jack cheese, sliced
2 garlic cloves, finely chopped
250ml/8fl oz/1 cup double
    (heavy) cream
2 large (US extra large) egg yolks
salt and ground black pepper

1 Preheat the oven to 190°C/375°F/ Gas 5. Cook the potatoes in boiling, lightly salted water for 3–4 minutes, then drain and set aside.

2 Thinly slice the leeks. Melt 25g/1oz/ 2 tbsp of the butter in a frying pan and fry the leeks gently over a low heat, stirring occasionally, until softened. Remove from the heat and season with pepper and stir in half the parsley and half the mixed herbs.

3 Melt the remaining butter. Line a 23cm/9in loose-bottomed metal cake tin (pan) with six sheets of filo pastry, brushing each layer with butter. Allow the edges of the pastry to overhang the tin.

4 Layer the potatoes, leeks and cheese in the tin, sprinkling a few herbs and the garlic between the layers. Season.

5 Flip the overhanging pastry over the filling and cover with another two sheets of filo pastry, tucking in the sides to fit, and brush with melted butter as before. Cover the pie loosely with foil and bake for 35 minutes. (Keep the remaining pastry covered with a plastic bag and a damp cloth.)

6 Meanwhile beat the cream, egg yolks and remaining herbs together. Make a hole in the centre of the pie and gradually pour in the eggs and cream.

7 Arrange the remaining pastry on top, teasing it into swirls and folds, then brush with melted butter.

8 Reduce the oven temperature to 180°C/350°F/Gas 4 and bake the pie for another 25–30 minutes, or until the top is golden and crisp. Allow to cool before serving.

COOK'S TIP
Serve this pie with a spicy tomato sauce. Fry 1 chopped onion in 15ml/1 tbsp olive oil for 3 minutes, add 1 chopped garlic clove and cook for 2 minutes. Stir in 400g/14oz can chopped tomatoes and 5ml/1 tsp hot chilli powder. Simmer for 15–20 minutes or until thickened.

VARIATIONS
• Reduce the quantity of leeks to 225g/8oz. Cook 1kg/2¼ lb washed spinach in a covered pan over a high heat for 3–4 minutes, shaking the pan frequently. Drain, chop and mix with the cooked leeks.
• Reduce the quantity of leeks to 225g/8oz. Blanch 450g/1lb small broccoli florets in boiling water for 1 minute. Drain and add to the leeks.
• For a punchy flavour, use blue cheese, such as Stilton or Danish Blue, instead of white cheese. Crumble the cheese rather than slicing it.

Baked Salmon with Watercress Sauce

A whole baked salmon makes a stunning centrepiece for a buffet. Baking it in foil is easier than poaching and yet the flesh has a similar melting quality. If you decorate the fish with thin slices of cucumber it will add a delicate touch to its appearance.

Serves 6 to 8

2–3kg/4½–6½lb salmon, cleaned
  with head and tail left on
3–5 spring onions (scallions),
  thinly sliced
1 lemon, thinly sliced
1 cucumber, thinly sliced
fresh dill sprigs, to garnish
lemon wedges, to serve
salt and ground black pepper

For the sauce
3 garlic cloves, chopped
200g/7oz watercress leaves,
  finely chopped
40g/1½oz/¾ cup finely chopped
  fresh tarragon
300g/11oz mayonnaise
15–30ml/1–2 tbsp freshly squeezed
  lemon juice
200g/7oz/scant 1 cup unsalted
  (sweet) butter

1 Preheat the oven to 180°C/350°F/ Gas 4. Rinse the salmon and lay it on a large piece of foil. Stuff the fish with the sliced spring onions and layer the lemon slices inside and around the fish, then sprinkle with salt and pepper.

2 Loosely fold the foil around the fish and fold the edges over to seal. Bake for about 1 hour.

3 Remove the fish from the oven and leave it to stand, still wrapped in the foil, for about 15 minutes. Then unwrap the foil parcel and leave the salmon to cool.

4 When the fish is cool, carefully lift it on to a large plate, still covered with lemon slices. Cover the fish tightly with clear film (plastic wrap) and chill for several hours in the refrigerator.

5 Use a blunt knife to lift up the edge of the skin and carefully peel the skin away from the flesh, avoiding tearing the flesh. Pull out any fins at the same time. Carefully turn over the salmon and repeat on the other side. Leave the head on for serving, if you wish. Discard the skin.

6 Arrange the cucumber slices in overlapping rows along the length of the fish, so that they look like large fish scales.

7 To make the sauce, put the garlic, watercress, tarragon, mayonnaise and lemon juice in a food processor or blender or a bowl, and process or mix to combine.

8 Melt the butter, then add to the watercress mixture, a little at a time, processing or stirring, until the butter has been incorporated and the sauce is thick and smooth. Cover and chill before serving.

9 Serve the fish, garnished with dill and lemon wedges, and the watercress sauce alongside.

COOK'S TIP
Do not prepare the sauce more than a few hours ahead of serving as the watercress will discolour it.

VARIATION
If you prefer to poach the fish rather than baking it you will need to use a fish kettle. Place the salmon on the rack, in the kettle. Cover with cold water and bring to a simmer, cook for 5–10 minutes per 450g/1lb until tender.

Cider-glazed Ham

A succulent gammon joint with a sweet cider glaze that looks impressive and tastes wonderful. Served with a zesty cranberry sauce, it is ideal for a Christmas or Thanksgiving buffet, but is equally well suited to any festive occasion.

Serves 8 to 10

2kg/4½ lb middle gammon joint
1 large or 2 small onions
about 30 whole cloves
3 bay leaves
10 black peppercorns
1.3 litres/2¼ pints/5⅔ cups
 medium-dry (hard) cider
45ml/3 tbsp soft light brown sugar
bunch of flat leaf parsley, to garnish

For the sauce
350g/12oz/3 cups cranberries
175g/6oz/¾ cup soft light brown sugar
grated rind and juice of 2 clementines
30ml/2 tbsp port

1 Weigh the gammon joint and calculate the cooking time at 20 minutes per 450g/1lb, then place it in a large casserole or pan. Stud the onion or onions with 5–10 of the cloves and add to the casserole or pan with the bay leaves and peppercorns.

VARIATION
Use clear honey in place of the soft brown sugar for the glaze and serve the ham with redcurrant sauce or jelly instead of the cranberry sauce.

2 Add 1.2 litres/2 pints/5 cups of the cider and enough water to just cover the ham. Heat until simmering and then carefully skim off the scum that rises to the surface using a large spoon. Start timing the cooking from the moment the stock begins to simmer.

3 Cover with a lid or foil and simmer gently for the calculated time. Towards the end of the cooking time, preheat the oven to 220°C/425°F/Gas 7.

4 Heat the sugar and remaining cider in a pan; stir until the sugar has dissolved. Simmer for 5 minutes to make a dark, sticky glaze. Remove the pan from the heat and leave to cool for 5 minutes.

COOK'S TIPS
• A large stock pot or preserving pan can be used for cooking the ham.
• Leave the ham until it is just cool enough to handle before removing the rind. Snip off the string, then carefully slice off the rind, leaving a thin, even layer of fat. Use a narrow-bladed, sharp knife for the best results.

5 Lift the ham out of the casserole or pan using a slotted spoon and a large fork. Carefully and evenly, cut the rind from the ham, then score the fat into a neat diamond pattern. Place the ham in a roasting pan or ovenproof dish.

6 Press a clove into the centre of each diamond, then carefully spoon over the glaze. Bake for 20–25 minutes, or until the fat is brown, glistening and crisp.

7 Simmer all the sauce ingredients in a heavy pan for 15–20 minutes, stirring frequently. Transfer the sauce to a jug.

8 Serve the ham hot or cold, garnished with parsley and with the cranberry sauce accompaniment.

Fillet of Beef with Ratatouille

This succulent beef is served cold with a colourful garlicky ratatouille.

Serves 8

675–900g/1½–2lb fillet of beef
45ml/3 tbsp olive oil
300ml/½ pint/1¼ cups aspic jelly, made
   up as packet instructions

For the marinade
30ml/2 tbsp sherry
30ml/2 tbsp olive oil
30ml/2 tbsp soy sauce
10ml/2 tsp grated fresh root ginger
   or 5ml/1 tsp ground ginger
2 garlic cloves, crushed

For the ratatouille
60ml/4 tbsp olive oil
1 onion, sliced
2–3 garlic cloves, crushed
1 large aubergine (eggplant), cubed
1 small red (bell) pepper, seeded
   and sliced
1 small green (bell) pepper, seeded
   and sliced
1 small yellow (bell) pepper, seeded
   and sliced
225g/8oz courgettes (zucchini), sliced
450g/1lb tomatoes, skinned
15ml/1 tbsp chopped fresh mixed herbs
30ml/2 tbsp French dressing
salt and ground black pepper

1 Mix all the marinade ingredients together and pour over the beef. Cover the dish with clear film (plastic wrap) and leave for 30 minutes.

2 Preheat the oven to 220°C/425°F/ Gas 7. Using a large slotted spoon, lift the fillet out of the marinade and pat it dry with kitchen paper. Heat the oil in a frying pan until smoking hot and then brown the beef all over to seal it.

3 Transfer the beef to a roasting pan and roast for 10–15 minutes, basting it occasionally with the marinade. Lift the beef out on to a large plate and leave it to cool.

4 Meanwhile, for the ratatouille, heat the oil in a large casserole and cook the onion and garlic over a low heat, until tender, without letting the onions become brown. Add the aubergine cubes to the casserole and cook for a further 5 minutes, until soft.

5 Add the sliced peppers and the courgettes and cook for 2 minutes more. Then add the tomatoes and chopped herbs, and season well with salt and pepper. Cook for a few minutes longer. Turn the ratatouille into a dish and set aside to cool. Drizzle with a little French dressing.

6 Slice the beef fillet and arrange overlapping slices on a large serving platter. Brush the slices of beef with a little cold aspic jelly that is just on the point of setting.

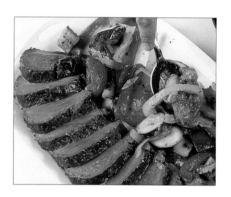

7 Leave the aspic jelly to set completely, then brush the beef slices with a second coat. Spoon the cooled ratatouille around the beef slices on the platter and serve immediately.

COOK'S TIP
Ratatouille is a traditional French recipe that is at its best when made with the choicest fresh ingredients. It makes a wonderful side dish for a buffet or can be eaten as a snack, as a vegetarian filling for jacket potatoes.

VARIATIONS
• Instead of marinating the beef in soy sauce and ginger, add 15ml/1 tbsp chopped fresh marjoram to the mixture, increase the quantity of sherry to 60ml/ 4 tbsp and add 15ml/1 tbsp crushed juniper berries.
• Use pork instead of beef and increase the roasting time to 20–30 minutes.

Rich Game Pie

Smart enough for a formal wedding buffet but also terrific for a stylish picnic, this rich game pie looks spectacular when baked in a fluted raised pie mould. Some specialist kitchen stores hire the moulds so you can avoid the expense of purchasing one; alternatively a 20cm/8in round deep, loose-bottomed tin can be used. Serve the pie garnished with salad leaves.

Serves 10

25g/1oz/2 tbsp butter
1 onion, finely chopped
2 garlic cloves, finely chopped
900g/2lb mixed boneless game meat,
    such as skinless pheasant and/or
    pigeon breast, venison and
    rabbit, diced
30ml/2 tbsp chopped mixed fresh
    herbs, such as parsley, thyme
    and marjoram
salt and ground black pepper

For the pâté
50g/2oz/¼ cup butter
2 garlic cloves, finely chopped
450g/1lb chicken livers, rinsed,
    trimmed and chopped
60ml/4 tbsp brandy
5ml/1 tsp ground mace

For the pastry
675g/1½lb/6 cups strong plain
    (all-purpose) flour
5ml/1 tsp salt
115ml/3½fl oz/scant ½ cup milk
115ml/3½fl oz/scant ½ cup water
115g/4oz/½ cup white cooking
    fat, diced
115g/4oz/½ cup butter, diced
beaten egg, to glaze

For the jelly
300ml/½ pint/1¼ cups game or
    beef consommé
2.5ml/½ tsp powdered gelatine

1 Melt the butter in a small pan until foaming, then add the onion and garlic, and cook until softened but not coloured. Remove from the heat and mix with the diced game meat and the chopped mixed herbs. Season well, cover and chill.

2 To make the pâté, melt the butter in a pan until foaming. Add the garlic and chicken livers and cook until the livers are just browned. Remove the pan from the heat and stir in the brandy and mace. Purée the mixture in a blender or food processor until smooth, then set aside and leave to cool completely.

3 To make the pastry, sift the flour and salt into a bowl and make a well in the centre. Place the milk and water in a pan. Add the white cooking fat and butter and heat gently until melted, then bring to the boil and remove from the heat as soon as the mixture begins to bubble. Pour the hot liquid into the well in the flour and beat until smooth. Cover and leave until the dough is cool enough to handle.

4 Preheat the oven to 200°C/400°F/Gas 6. Roll out two-thirds of the pastry and use to line a 23cm/9in raised pie mould. Press the pastry into the flutes in the mould and around the edge. Patch any thin areas with offcuts (scraps) from the top edge. Spoon in half the mixture and press it down evenly. Add the pâté and then top with the remaining game.

5 Roll out the remaining pastry to form a lid. Brush the edge of the pastry lining the tin with a little water and cover the pie with the pastry lid. Trim off excess pastry from around the edge. Pinch the edges together to seal in the filling. Make two holes in the centre of the lid and glaze with egg. Use pastry trimmings to roll out leaves to garnish the pie. Brush with egg.

6 Bake the pie for 20 minutes, then cover it with foil and cook for a further 10 minutes. Reduce the oven temperature to 150°C/300°F/Gas 2. Glaze the pie again with beaten egg and cook for a further 1½ hours, with the top covered loosely with foil.

7 Remove the pie from the oven and leave it to stand for 15 minutes. Increase the oven temperature to 200°C/400°F/Gas 6. Stand the tin on a baking sheet and remove the sides. Quickly glaze the sides of the pie with beaten egg and cover the top with foil, then cook for a final 15 minutes to brown the sides. Leave to cool completely, then chill the pie overnight.

8 To make the jelly, heat the game or beef consommé in a small pan until just beginning to bubble, whisk in the gelatine until dissolved and leave to cool until just setting. Using a small funnel, carefully pour the jellied consommé into the holes in the pie. Chill until set. This pie will keep in the refrigerator for up to 3 days.

Turkey and Cranberry Pie

This is ideal for using up leftovers and the cranberries add a tart layer to this attractive pie. It needs to be made the day before, and it can even be frozen in advance.

Serves 8

450g/1lb pork sausage meat
  (bulk sausage)
450g/1lb/2 cups minced (ground) pork
15ml/1 tbsp ground coriander
15ml/1 tbsp mixed dried herbs
finely grated rind of 2 large oranges
10ml/2 tsp grated fresh root ginger or
  2.5ml/½ tsp ground ginger
450g/1lb turkey breast fillets, skinned
115g/4oz/1 cup fresh cranberries
salt and ground black pepper

For the pastry
450g/1lb/4 cups plain (all-purpose) flour
5ml/1 tsp salt
150g/5oz/10 tbsp white cooking fat
150ml/¼ pint/⅔ cup mixed milk and
  water

To finish
1 egg, beaten
300ml/½ pint/1¼ cups aspic jelly, made
  up as packet instructions

1 Preheat the oven to 180°C/350°F/ Gas 4. Place a large baking tray in the oven to preheat. In a large bowl, mix together the sausage meat, minced pork, coriander, mixed dried herbs, orange rind and ginger with plenty of salt and ground black pepper.

2 To make the pastry, put the flour into a large bowl with the salt. Heat the fat in a small pan with the milk and water until just beginning to boil. Set aside and allow to cool slightly.

3 Using a spoon, stir the liquid into the flour until a stiff dough forms. Turn on to a worksurface and knead until smooth. Cut one-third off the dough for the lid, wrap it in clear film (plastic wrap), and keep it in a warm place.

4 Roll out the large piece of dough on a floured surface and line the base and sides of a well-greased 20cm/8in loose-bottomed, springform cake pan. Work the dough while it is warm, as it will crack and break if it is left to get cold.

5 Thinly slice the turkey fillets and put between two pieces of clear film and flatten with a rolling pin to a 3mm/⅛in thickness. Spoon half the pork mixture into the base of the tin, pressing it well into the edges. Cover with half of the turkey slices and then the cranberries, followed by the remaining turkey and finally the rest of the pork mixture.

6 Roll out the rest of the dough and cover the filling, trimming any excess and sealing the edges with beaten egg. Make a steam hole in the lid and decorate with pastry trimmings. Brush with beaten egg. Bake for 2 hours. Cover the pie with foil if it gets too brown. Place the pie on a wire rack to cool. When cold, use a funnel to fill the pie with aspic jelly. Allow to set for a few hours before unmoulding the pie.

COOK'S TIPS
• Stand the springform pan on a baking tray with a shallow rim to catch any juices that may seep from the pie during baking.
• Leave the pie to cool in the pan until the pastry has firmed up slightly before transferring it to a wire rack.

stylish salads

A repertoire of exciting salads is every cook's standby for colourful first courses, refreshing side dishes or buffet pizzazz.

New York Deli Coleslaw

The key to a good coleslaw is a zesty dressing and an interesting selection of vegetables. Serve at barbecues, picnics or buffets.

Serves 6 to 8

1 large white or green cabbage, very
   thinly sliced
3–4 carrots, coarsely grated
½ red (bell) pepper, chopped
½ green (bell) pepper, chopped
1–2 celery sticks, finely chopped or
   5–10ml/1–2 tsp celery seeds
1 onion, chopped
2–3 handfuls of raisins or sultanas
   (golden raisins)
45ml/3 tbsp white wine vinegar or
   cider vinegar
60–90ml/4–6 tbsp sugar, to taste
175–250ml/6–8fl oz/¾–1 cup
   mayonnaise, to bind
salt and ground black pepper

1 Put the cabbage, carrots, peppers, celery or celery seeds, onion, and raisins or sultanas in a salad bowl and mix to combine well. Add the vinegar, sugar, salt and ground black pepper and toss together. Leave to stand for about 1 hour.

COOK'S TIP
The salad can be prepared beforehand to the end of step 1 and chilled overnight. Next day, it can be dressed with the mayonnaise before serving.

2 Stir enough mayonnaise into the salad to lightly bind the ingredients together. Taste the salad for seasoning and sweet-and-sour flavour, adding more sugar, salt and pepper if necessary. Chill for about 1 hour.

3 Drain off any excess liquid that has formed before serving.

VARIATION
Use low-fat fromage frais or crème fraîche for a lighter dressing.

Potato Salad with Egg, Mayonnaise and Olives

This version of potato salad includes a mustard mayonnaise, chopped eggs and green olives.

Serves 6 to 8

1kg/2¼lb waxy salad potatoes, cleaned
1 red, brown or white onion,
   finely chopped
2–3 celery sticks, finely chopped
60–90ml/4–6 tbsp chopped parsley
15–20 pimiento-stuffed olives, halved
3 hard-boiled eggs, chopped
60ml/4 tbsp extra virgin olive oil
60ml/4 tbsp white wine vinegar
15–30ml/1–2 tbsp mild or
   wholegrain mustard
celery seeds, to taste (optional)
175–250ml/6–8fl oz/¾–1 cup
   mayonnaise
salt and ground black pepper
paprika, to garnish

1 Cook the potatoes in a pan of salted boiling water until tender. Drain, return to the pan and leave for 2–3 minutes to cool and dry a little.

2 When the potatoes are cool enough to handle but still warm, cut them into chunks and place in a salad bowl.

VARIATION
Instead of potatoes, use 400g/14oz cooked macaroni.

3 Sprinkle the potatoes with salt and pepper, then add the onion, celery, parsley, olives and the chopped eggs to the salad bowl.

4 In a jug (pitcher), combine the olive oil, vinegar, mustard and celery seeds, if using. Pour over the salad and toss to combine thoroughly. Add enough mayonnaise to bind the salad together. Chill for about 1 hour before serving, sprinkled with a little paprika.

Peruvian Salad

This really is a spectacular-looking salad. If you serve it in a deep, glass salad bowl, the guests can then see the various layers of rice and green salad leaves, topped by the bright colours of the peppers, corn, eggs and olives.

Serves 8

*450g/1lb/4 cups cooked long grain
  brown or white rice
30ml/2 tbsp chopped fresh parsley
2 red (bell) peppers
2 onions, sliced
olive oil, for sprinkling
250g/9oz green beans, halved
115g/4oz/²/3 cup baby corn
8 quail's eggs, hard-boiled
75g/3oz Spanish ham, cut into
  thin slices (optional)
2 small avocados
lemon juice, for sprinkling
150g/5oz mixed salad
30ml/2 tbsp capers
about 20 stuffed olives, halved*

For the dressing
*2 garlic cloves, crushed
120ml/4fl oz/¹/2 cup olive oil
90ml/6 tbsp sunflower oil
60ml/4 tbsp lemon juice
90ml/6 tbsp natural (plain) yogurt
5ml/1 tsp mustard
5ml/1 tsp granulated sugar
salt and ground black pepper*

1 Make the dressing by placing all the ingredients in a bowl and whisking with a fork until smooth. Alternatively, shake the ingredients together in a screwtop jar.

COOK'S TIP
To hard-boil quail's eggs, place them in a pan of simmering water, bring the water back to simmering point and cook for 4 minutes. Drain the eggs and rinse in cold water, then shell.

2 Put the cooked rice into a large bowl and spoon in half the dressing. Add the chopped parsley, stir well and set aside.

3 Cut the peppers in half, remove the seeds and pith, then place the halves, cut side down, in a small roasting pan. Add the onion rings. Sprinkle the onion with a little olive oil, place the pan under a hot grill (broiler) and grill (broil) for 5–6 minutes, or until the peppers blacken and blister and the onion turns golden. You may need to stir the onion once or twice so that it grills evenly.

4 Stir the onion in with the rice. Put the pepper in a bowl, cover and leave until cool. Peel the peppers and cut the flesh into thin strips.

5 Cook the green beans in boiling water for 2 minutes, then add the corn and cook for 1–2 minutes more, until tender. Drain both vegetables, refresh them under cold water, then drain again. Place in a large mixing bowl and add the red pepper strips, quail's eggs and ham, if using.

6 Peel each avocado, remove the stone (pit), and cut the flesh into slices or chunks. Sprinkle with the lemon juice. Put the salad in a separate mixing bowl, add the avocado and mix lightly. Arrange the salad on top of the rice.

7 Stir about 45ml/3 tbsp of the remaining dressing into the green bean and pepper mixture. Pile this on top of the salad.

8 Sprinkle the capers and stuffed olives on top and serve the salad with the remaining dressing.

VARIATION
Use couscous instead of rice. Place in a bowl and cover with 2.5cm/1in boiling water. Leave to stand for 10–15 minutes.

Moroccan Orange, Onion and Olive Salad

This is a refreshing salad to add to a selection of buffet dishes.

Serves 6

5 large oranges
90g/3½oz/scant 1 cup black olives
1 red onion, thinly sliced
1 large fennel bulb, thinly sliced,
*   feathery tops reserved*
15ml/1 tbsp chopped fresh mint, plus
*   a few extra sprigs to garnish*
15ml/1 tbsp chopped fresh coriander
*   (cilantro), plus extra to garnish*
60ml/4 tbsp olive oil
10ml/2 tsp lemon juice
2.5ml/½ tsp ground toasted
*   coriander seeds*
2.5ml/½ tsp orange flower water
salt and ground black pepper

1 Peel the oranges with a sharp knife, making sure you remove all the white pith, and cut them into 5mm/¼in slices. Remove any pips (seeds) and work over a bowl to catch all the orange juice. Set the juice aside for adding to the salad dressing.

2 Stone (pit) the olives, if you like. In a bowl, toss the orange slices, onion and fennel together with the olives, chopped fresh mint and coriander.

3 Make the dressing: in a bowl or jug (pitcher), whisk together the olive oil, 15ml/1 tbsp of the reserved fresh orange juice and the lemon juice. Add the ground toasted coriander seeds and season to taste with a little salt and pepper. Whisk thoroughly to mix.

4 Toss the dressing into the salad, cover and leave to stand in a cool place for 30–60 minutes.

5 To serve, drain off any excess dressing and place the salad in a serving dish or bowl. Sprinkle with the chopped herbs and reserved fennel tops, and sprinkle with the orange flower water.

Tomato, Mozzarella and Red Onion Salad with Basil and Caper Dressing

Sweet tomatoes and the heady scent of basil capture the essence of summer in this simple salad.

Serves 8

10 large ripe tomatoes
4 small packets buffalo mozzarella
*   cheese, drained and sliced*
2 small red onions, chopped
fresh basil and parsley sprigs, to garnish

For the dressing

1 small garlic clove, peeled
25g/1oz/1 cup fresh basil
60ml/4 tbsp chopped fresh flat
*   leaf parsley*
45ml/3 tbsp salted capers, rinsed
5ml/1 tsp mustard
150ml/¼ pint/⅔ cup extra virgin
*   olive oil*
15ml/1tbsp balsamic vinegar
salt and ground black pepper

1 First make the dressing. Put the garlic, basil, parsley, half the capers and the mustard in a food processor or blender and process briefly to chop. Then, with the motor running, gradually pour in the olive oil through the feeder tube to make a smooth purée with a dressing consistency. Add the balsamic vinegar to taste and season with ground black pepper. Alternatively, the dressing can be made by pounding the ingredients in a mortar and adding the oil by hand.

2 Slice the tomatoes thinly. Arrange the tomato and mozzarella slices overlapping alternately on a large plate. Sprinkle the onion over the top and season with a little pepper.

3 Drizzle the dressing over the salad, then sprinkle a few basil leaves, parsley sprigs and the remaining capers on top.

4 Leave the salad to marinate for 10–15 minutes for the flavours to develop before serving.

Country Pasta Salad

Colourful, tasty and nutritious, this is the ideal pasta salad for a picnic.

Serves 6

300g/11oz/2¾ cups dried fusilli
150g/5oz green beans, trimmed and
    cut into 5cm/2in lengths
1 potato, about 150g/5oz, diced
200g/7oz baby tomatoes, hulled
    and halved
2 spring onions (scallions), chopped
90g/3½oz/scant 1¼ cups Parmesan
    cheese, diced or coarsely shaved
6–8 pitted black olives, cut into rings
15–30ml/1–2 tbsp capers, to taste

For the dressing
90ml/6 tbsp extra virgin olive oil
15ml/1 tbsp balsamic vinegar
15ml/1 tbsp chopped fresh flat
    leaf parsley
salt and ground black pepper

1 Cook the pasta according to the instructions on the packet. Drain it into a colander, rinse under cold running water until cold, then shake the colander to remove as much water as possible. Leave to drain and dry, shaking the colander occasionally so that it does not stick.

2 Cook the beans and diced potato in a pan of salted boiling water for 5–6 minutes, or until tender. Drain and leave to cool.

3 Make the dressing. Put all the ingredients in a large bowl with salt and pepper to taste and whisk well until thoroughly combined.

4 Add the baby tomatoes, spring onions, Parmesan, olive rings and capers to the dressing, then the cold pasta, beans and potato. Toss well to mix all the ingredients. Cover the salad and leave to stand for about 30 minutes. Season to taste with salt and pepper before serving.

Salad with Watermelon and Feta Cheese

The combination of sweet and juicy watermelon with salty feta cheese was inspired by the Turkish tradition of eating watermelon with salty white cheese in the hot summer months. It is ideal for barbecues and picnics.

Serves 6 to 8

30–45ml/2–3 tbsp extra virgin olive oil
juice of ½ lemon
5ml/1 tsp vinegar of choice
sprinkling of fresh thyme
pinch of ground cumin
4 large slices of watermelon, chilled
1 frisée lettuce, core removed
130g/4½oz feta cheese, preferably
  sheep's milk feta, cut into
  bitesize pieces
handful of lightly toasted
  pumpkin seeds
handful of sunflower seeds
10–15 black olives

1 Pour the extra virgin olive oil, lemon juice and vinegar into a bowl or jug (pitcher). Add the fresh thyme and ground cumin, and whisk until well combined. Set the dressing aside until you are ready to serve the salad.

2 Cut the rind off the watermelon and remove as many seeds as possible.

COOK'S TIP
Use plump black Mediterranean olives such as kalamata for this recipe or other shiny, dry-cured black olives.

3 Cut the flesh into bitesize triangular-shaped chunks.

4 Put the lettuce leaves in a bowl, pour over the dressing and toss together. Arrange the leaves on a serving dish or individual plates and add the watermelon, feta cheese, pumpkin and sunflower seeds and black olives. Serve the salad immediately.

VARIATION
Use Galia, cantaloupe or Charentais melon instead of the watermelon.

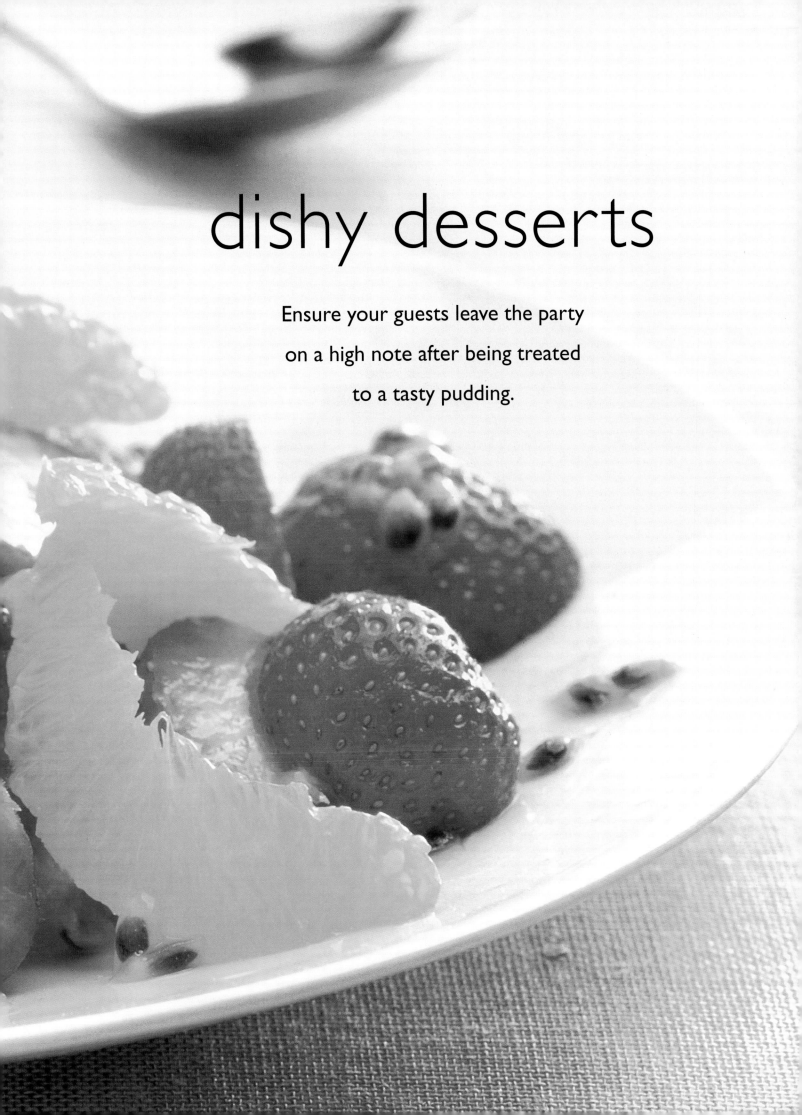

dishy desserts

Ensure your guests leave the party

on a high note after being treated

to a tasty pudding.

Tropical Scented Red and Orange Fruit Salad

This fresh fruit salad, with its bright colour and exotic flavour, is perfect after a rich, heavy meal or on the buffet table. It is also a refreshing dish to serve at a summer picnic or barbecue.

Serves 4 to 6

350–400g/12–14oz/3–3½ cups
  strawberries, hulled and halved
3 oranges, peeled and segmented
3 small blood oranges, peeled
  and segmented
1–2 passion fruit
120ml/4fl oz/½ cup dry white wine
sugar, to taste

1 Put the strawberries and oranges into a serving bowl. Halve the passion fruit and spoon the flesh into the bowl.

2 Pour the wine over the fruit and add sugar to taste. Toss gently and then chill until ready to serve.

COOK'S TIP
Omit the white wine if you wish and replace with orange or tropical juice.

VARIATION
Other fruits that can be added include pear, kiwi fruit and banana.

Iced Lime Cheesecake

4 Press the cottage cheese through a sieve into a bowl. Beat in the mascarpone cheese, then the lime syrup. By hand: lightly whip the cream and then fold into the cheese mixture. Pour into a shallow container and freeze until thick. If you are using an ice cream maker, add the lightly-whipped cream and churn in an ice cream maker until thick.

5 Meanwhile, cut a slice off either end of each of the remaining limes, stand them on a board and slice off the skins. Cut them into very thin slices.

6 Arrange the lime slices around the sides of the tin, pressing them against the paper.

7 Pour the cheese mixture over the biscuit base in the tin and level the surface. Cover and freeze the cheesecake overnight.

8 About 1 hour before you are going to serve the cheesecake, carefully transfer it to a serving plate and put it in the refrigerator to soften slightly.

This frozen dessert has a deliciously tangy, sweet flavour but needs no gelatine to set the filling, unlike most unbaked cheesecakes. It is not difficult to prepare and an added advantage is that it can be made several days beforehand.

Serves 10

175g/6oz almond biscuits (cookies)
65g/2½oz/5 tbsp unsalted
   (sweet) butter
8 limes
115g/4oz/generous ½ cup caster
   (superfine) sugar
90ml/6 tbsp water
200g/7oz/scant 1 cup cottage cheese
250g/9oz/generous 1 cup mascarpone
   cheese
300ml/½ pint/1¼ cups double
   (heavy) cream

1 Lightly grease the sides of a 20cm/8in springform cake tin (pan) and line with a strip of baking parchment. Break up the almond biscuits slightly, put them in a strong plastic bag and crush them with a rolling pin.

2 Melt the butter in a small pan and stir in the biscuit crumbs until evenly combined. Spoon the mixture into the tin and pack it down with the back of a spoon. Freeze the biscuit mixture while you make the filling.

3 Finely grate the rind and squeeze the juice from five of the limes. Heat the sugar and water in a small pan, stirring until the sugar dissolves. Bring to the boil and boil for 2 minutes without stirring, then remove the syrup from the heat, stir in the lime juice and rind and leave to cool.

Coconut and Coffee Trifle

Serve this lavish dessert in a large glass bowl for maximum impact.

Serves 6 to 8

For the coffee sponge
45ml/3 tbsp strong-flavoured
    ground coffee
45ml/3 tbsp near-boiling water
2 eggs
50g/2oz/¼ cup soft dark brown sugar
40g/1½oz/⅓ cup self-raising
    (self-rising) flour, sifted
25ml/1½ tbsp hazelnut or
    sunflower oil

For the coconut custard
400ml/14fl oz/1⅔ cup coconut milk
3 eggs
40g/1½oz/3 tbsp caster
    (superfine) sugar
10ml/2 tsp cornflour (cornstarch)

For the filling and topping
2 medium bananas
60ml/4 tbsp coffee liqueur
300ml/½ pint/1¼ cups double
    (heavy) cream
30ml/2 tbsp icing (confectioners')
    sugar, sifted
ribbons of fresh coconut, to decorate

1 Preheat the oven to 160°C/325°F/Gas 3. Grease and line an 18cm/7in baking tin (pan) with baking parchment.

2 Put the coffee in a jug (pitcher). Pour the hot water over and leave for 4 minutes. Strain through a fine sieve.

3 Whisk the eggs and soft dark brown sugar in a large bowl.

4 Gently fold in the flour, followed by 15ml/1 tbsp of the coffee and the oil. Spoon the mixture into the tin and bake for 20 minutes, until firm. Turn out on to a wire rack, remove the lining paper and leave to cool.

5 To make the coconut custard, heat the coconut milk in a pan until it is almost boiling.

6 Whisk the eggs, sugar and cornflour until frothy. Pour on the hot coconut milk. Add to the pan and heat gently, stirring for 1–2 minutes, until the custard thickens, but do not boil.

7 Set the custard aside to cool for about 10 minutes, stirring occasionally.

8 Cut the coffee sponge into 5cm/2in squares and arrange in the base of a large glass bowl. Slice the bananas and arrange on top of the sponge. Drizzle the coffee liqueur on top. Pour the custard over and leave until cold.

9 Whip the cream with the remaining coffee and icing sugar until soft peaks form. Spoon the cream over the custard. Cover and chill for several hours. Sprinkle with ribbons of fresh coconut before serving.

COOK'S TIP
To make coconut ribbons, use a vegetable peeler to cut thin ribbons from the flesh of a fresh coconut, or buy desiccated (dry unsweetened shredded) coconut and toast until it is a pale golden brown colour.

VARIATION
Coffee liqueurs such as Tia Maria or Kahlúa can be used in the trifle or if you prefer use brandy or whisky.

Chocolate Truffles

These irresistible, melt-in-the-mouth truffles will make a dainty addition to the buffet table as a dessert or as an after-dinner treat. Use a good quality chocolate with a high percentage of cocoa solids to give a real depth of flavour.

Makes 20 to 30

175ml/6fl oz/¾ cup double
   (heavy) cream
1 egg yolk, beaten
275g/10oz plain (semisweet)
   Belgian chocolate, chopped
25g/1oz/2 tbsp unsalted (sweet)
   butter, cut into pieces
30–45ml/2–3 tbsp brandy (optional)

For the coatings
cocoa powder (unsweetened)
finely chopped pistachio nuts
   or hazelnuts
400g/14oz plain (semisweet), milk
   or white chocolate, or a mixture

1 Bring the cream to the boil, then remove the pan from the heat and beat in the egg yolk. Add the chocolate, then stir until melted and smooth. Stir in the butter and the brandy, if using, then pour into a bowl and leave to cool. Cover and chill in the refrigerator for 6–8 hours.

COOK'S TIP
Chocolate truffles will delight guests at a drinks party – serve them with coffee to follow all the savoury bites.

2 Line a large baking sheet with baking parchment. Using a very small ice-cream scoop or two teaspoons, form the chocolate mixture into 20–30 balls and place on the parchment. Chill if the mixture becomes too soft.

3 To coat the truffles with cocoa, sift some powder into a small bowl, drop in the truffles, one at a time, and roll to coat well. To coat them with nuts, roll the truffles in finely chopped pistachio nuts or hazelnuts.

4 To coat with chocolate, freeze the truffles for at least 1 hour. In a small bowl, melt the plain, milk or white chocolate over a pan of barely simmering water, stirring until melted and smooth, then allow to cool slightly.

5 Using a fork, dip the frozen truffles into the cooled chocolate, one at a time, tapping the fork on the edge of the bowl to shake off the excess. Place on a baking sheet lined with baking parchment and chill. If the melted chocolate thickens, reheat until smooth. All the truffles can be stored, well wrapped, in the refrigerator for up to 10 days.

Mint Chocolate Meringues

Omit the alcohol and these mini meringues are perfect for a child's birthday party.

Makes about 50

2 egg whites
115g/4oz/generous ½ cup caster (superfine) sugar
50g/2oz chocolate mint sticks, chopped
cocoa powder (unsweetened), sifted (optional)

For the filling
150ml/¼ pint/⅔ cup double (heavy) or whipping cream
5–10ml/1–2 tsp crème de menthe, or mint essence

1 Preheat the oven to 110°C/225°F/ Gas ¼. Line two or three baking sheets with baking parchment. Whisk the egg whites until stiff, then gradually whisk in the sugar until it is thick and glossy.

2 Fold in the chopped mint sticks and then place teaspoons of the mixture on the prepared baking sheets.

3 Bake for 1 hour or until crisp. Remove from the oven and allow to cool, then dust with cocoa, if using.

4 Lightly whip the cream until it stands in soft peaks and stir in the crème de menthe or mint essence. Use the cream to sandwich the meringues together in pairs just before serving.

Index